MATH SERIES

by Stan VerNooy

Book cover design by Kathy Kifer

515

To my sons: Justin and Dean, and Dean and Justin

Published by:
Garlic Press
100 Hillview Lane #2
Eugene, OR 97408

ISBN 0-931993-67-9
Order Number GP-067

Introduction

Calculus AB, Volume 2 primarily covers integral calculus and the applications of integrals. Differential calculus was covered in Volume 1. It is assumed in this book that the reader is familiar with the material in Volume 1, as well as the material in Straight Forward Algebra, Straight Forward Trigonometry, and Straight Forward Pre-Calculus.

Volumes 1 and 2 of Straight Forward Calculus AB are together intended to cover all the material required for the Advanced Placement in Calculus AB. The more rigorous theoretical foundations of calculus, as well as advanced topics such as the convergence of series, are part of Calculus BC and are not covered in this book.

095650

Contents

Antiderivatives

The primary topic of **Calculus AB, Volume 1** was derivatives. We start with a function, and then we find its derivative. It turns out that it is just as important to be able to start with a function f(x), and then find a function whose derivative is f(x). This process is generally more difficult than finding a derivative, for several reasons which will be seen in the material ahead.

Part 1 Basic Antidifferentiation Formulas

If r(x) = s'(x), then, as we know, r(x) is the *derivative* of s(x). We can also say, in this case, that s(x) is an *antiderivative* of r(x). (Notice that we say *an* antiderivative, not *the* antiderivative. That was no accident! Explanation soon.) Just as the process of finding the derivative of a function is called differentiation, the process of finding an antiderivative for a function is called *antidifferentiation*.

Why we say "an antiderivative" instead of "the antiderivative":

Suppose f(x) is the constant function -4. We want to find an antiderivative for f(x). We ask ourselves: How could we have got the constant -4 by differentiating a function? One answer is that we would have got -4 if the original function had been -4x (because the derivative of -4x is -4). However, we could have started with the function -4x + 22, or -4x - π, and the derivative would still have been -4. In fact, if the original function is -4x + C, where C is any constant (positive or negative), then the derivative will be -4. Therefore f(x) = -4 has an infinite number of antiderivatives, because there is an infinite number of possibilities for C in the expression -4x + C.

An important fact relating to the discussion above is:

> If f(x) and g(x) have the same derivative, then
> $$f(x) = g(x) + C$$
> for some constant C.

Therefore we know that if f(x) is the constant function -4, then any antiderivative of f(x) is -4x + C, for some constant C.

Because there are many possible antiderivatives for the constant function -4, we refer to -4x + C as the <u>indefinite integral</u> of -4. In other words, the indefinite integral of f(x) is an antiderivative of f(x), with a "+ C" attached at the end. The symbol for the indefinite integral of f(x) is $\int f(x)dx$—kind of an elongated "S" in front of the function, with the letters "dx" after it. The meaning of "dx" is that we want to antidifferentiate *with respect to x*, just as the "dx" in the expression $\frac{dy}{dx}$ meant that we were differentiating with respect to x. The word "integral" also gives rise to the verb "integrate" which means the same thing as "antidifferentiate".

Some of the most basic formulas for finding indefinite integrals are given below:

$$\int (f(x) + g(x))dx = \int f(x)dx + \int g(x)dx$$

In other words, we can antidifferentiate term by term, just as we could differentiate term by term.

$$\int k\,(x)dx = k \int f(x)dx \quad \text{for any constant k.}$$

In other words, we can antidifferentiate a constant times a function by antidifferentiating the function without the constant multiple, and then multiplying by the constant at the end of the process. This is to be expected, since we were able to do the same thing when differentiating.

$$\int a\,dx = ax + C \quad \text{for any constant a.}$$

$$\int ax^n dx = \frac{ax^{n+1}}{n+1} + C \quad \text{for any constants a and n, with } n \neq -1.$$

This rule is just the converse of the power rule for differentiating. Notice that if we differentiate the right-hand side of the expression above, we get ax^n, just as we should.

$$\int \frac{a}{x}dx = \int ax^{-1}dx = a\,\ln|x| + C.$$

We use the absolute value sign because only positive numbers are in the domain of the ln function. If we restrict x to positive values, then the absolute value signs make no difference.

$$\int e^{ax+b}dx = \frac{e^{ax+b}}{a} + C \quad \text{for any constants a and b, with } a \neq 0.$$

2

We also have the obvious formulas for antiderivatives of some trigonometric functions:

$$\int \cos x\, dx = \sin x + C$$

$$\int -\sin x\, dx = \cos x + C$$

$$\int \sec^2 x\, dx = \tan x + C$$

$$\int \sec x \tan x\, dx = \sec x + C$$

$$\int -\csc x \cot x\, dx = \csc x + C$$

$$\int -\csc^2 x\, dx = \cot x + C$$

These are, of course, just the opposite of the differentiation formulas introduced earlier.

We also have integral formulas for the derivatives of the inverse trigonometric functions:

$$\int \frac{1}{\sqrt{1-x^2}}\, dx = \sin^{-1} x + C$$

$$\int \frac{-1}{\sqrt{1-x^2}}\, dx = \cos^{-1} x + C$$

$$\int \frac{1}{x^2+1}\, dx = \tan^{-1} x + C$$

$$\int \frac{1}{\sqrt{x^2-1}}\, dx = \sec^{-1} x + C$$

$$\int \frac{-1}{|x|\sqrt{x^2-1}}\, dx = \csc^{-1} x + C$$

$$\int \frac{-1}{x^2+1}\, dx = \cot^{-1} x + C$$

3

You Might As Well Know It Now:

> Antidifferentiation has no product rule, no quotient rule, no chain rule, and no general power rule. That doesn't mean that products, quotients, and composite functions don't have antiderivatives. It just means that we have to work harder to find the antiderivatives, and there is no straightforward formula which works every time. In some cases, there is no antiderivative which can be expressed as any combination of functions we are familiar with. For example, the function
>
> $$f(x) = e^{x^2}$$
>
> cannot be integrated to yield any combination of exponential, logarithmic, trigonometric, polynomial, and/or rational functions.

Examples:

> Find the following indefinite integrals:
>
> 1. $\int \left(2x^2 - \frac{2}{x^2} \right) dx$
>
> 2. $\int \frac{-\pi}{x} dx$
>
> 3. $\int 5e^{3-2x} dx$
>
> 4. $\int \frac{3x^4 - 4x^3 + 5x^2 - 6x + 7}{x} dx$
>
> 5. $\int \left(\sec^2 x + \frac{4}{3x} \right) dx$
>
> SOLUTIONS:
>
> 1. The function can be rewritten as $2x^3 - 2x^{-3}$. According to the formula given earlier, therefore,
>
> $$\int \left(2x^3 - 2x^2 \right) dx = \frac{2x^4}{4} - \frac{2x^{-2}}{-2} + C = \frac{x^4}{2} + x^{-2} + C.$$
>
> 2. Remember that π is a constant! The function in this case can be rewritten as πx^{-1}. Therefore, a formula given earlier shows that the answer is:
>
> $$\pi \ln |x| + C.$$
>
> 3. The earlier formula for the antiderivative of "e" functions (when the exponent is a linear function of x) can be used here. The answer is
>
> $$\frac{-5}{2} e^{3-2x} + C.$$

4

4. This function looks intimidating until we realize that we can separate it into a sum of five fractions, each of which can be reduced and simplified:

$$\frac{3x^4}{x} - \frac{4x^3}{x} + \frac{5x^2}{x} - \frac{6x}{x} + \frac{7}{x} = 3x^3 - 4x^2 + 5x - 6 + 7x^{-1}$$

Now, the formula for the integral of x to a power gives the answer:

$$\frac{3}{4}x^4 - \frac{4}{3}x^3 + \frac{5}{2}x^2 - 6x + 7\ln|x| + C$$

Notice that this trick would not have been available if the <u>denominator</u> had had five terms and the numerator only one. This observation leads to an idea which will come up again: *We always prefer a complicated numerator and a simple denominator rather than the reverse.*

5. The second term of the function can be rewritten as $\frac{4}{3}x^{-1}$.
Since we know that $\int \sec^2 x\, dx = \tan x + C$ and $\int x^{-1}\, dx = \ln|x| + C$, the answer is

$$\tan x + \frac{4}{3}\ln|x| + C.$$

One might think that the answer should be $\tan x + C + \frac{4}{3}\ln|x| + C$ or $\tan x + \frac{4}{3}\ln|x| + 2C$, but C can be any arbitrary constant, including the sum of the two previous C's. So a single "+ C" includes all the same possibilities that "+ 2C" includes.

Antiderivatives. Exercise 1.

In Problems 1-10, find an expression which describes all antiderivatives of the given function.

1. e^{x+2}

2. $\frac{-2}{\sqrt{1-x^2}}$

3. $\frac{\sqrt{x}}{3}$

4. $\frac{-3}{5x}$

5. $e^{\frac{x}{2}-6}$

6. $\frac{4}{5x^2+5}$

7. $x^{-\frac{2}{3}}$

8. $\frac{x^5}{4}$

9. $\frac{3}{5}\sec^2 x$

10. $\sqrt{x^3}$

In problems 11-25, find the indefinite integral of the given function.

11. $\frac{e}{x}$

12. $-6x^{11}$

13. $\frac{\sin x}{4}$

14. $\frac{2}{3x^5}$

15. $\frac{1}{x}$

16. $\frac{-2x^4}{7}$

17. $\frac{1}{x\sqrt{x^2-1}}$

18. $7x^{\frac{1}{3}}$

19. $\frac{1}{-5x}$

20. $-\csc x \, \cot x$

21. $\frac{-2}{x^3}$

22. $\frac{2x^{-\frac{5}{4}}}{5}$

23. $-2e^{\frac{3x}{2}-8}$

24. x^{-5}

25. $4x^{-\frac{2}{3}}$

In problems 26-40, evaluate the given integral.

26. $\int x \, dx$

27. $\int -2\sec^2 x \, dx$

28. $\int \frac{1}{3x^4} dx$

29. $\int \frac{-2}{5\sqrt[3]{x^4}} dx$

30. $\int e^{7x+\pi} dx$

31. $\int \frac{1}{\sqrt{4-4x^2}} dx$

32. $\int \frac{7x^{\frac{7}{5}}}{5} dx$

33. $\int \left(\frac{2}{x^2+1} - \frac{3}{x} \right) dx$

34. $\int \left(\frac{e^{\frac{1}{4}x-2}}{3} + x^{-\frac{7}{3}} \right) dx$

35. $\int \left(\frac{-2\cos t}{3} + \frac{4}{t} \right) dt$

36. $\int \left(5x^4 - \frac{4}{3x^3} \right) dx$

37. $\int \frac{y^3+4y^2-3\sqrt{y}+2}{5y} dy$

38. $\int \left(x^{-2} + \frac{4}{\sqrt{x}} - x^2 \right) dx$

39. $\int \left(2\sin t + \frac{1}{3t^3} - \frac{3}{5\sqrt{t^5}} \right) dt$

40. $\int \left(-e^{5x} + \frac{1}{3x^2+3} + \frac{2\sqrt[3]{x}}{9} \right) dx$

6

Part 2

Finding the Constant

In the previous part, we learned that a given function has an infinite number of possible antiderivatives; hence the "+ C" we put at the end of the indefinite integral. However, if we know the value of the antiderivative for even one value of x, we can establish the actual value of C.

Examples:

1. $f'(x) = 2x - 3$, and $f(0) = 4$. Find $f(x)$.

2. Find the function whose derivative is $0.6e^{3t}$, and which has the value 5.2 when $t = 0$.

3. Suppose $g'(x) = 2 \sin x$, and $g(\pi) = 0$. Find $g\left(\frac{2\pi}{3}\right)$.

SOLUTIONS:

1. From the material in the previous part, we know that all antiderivatives of $2x - 3$ have the form $x^2 - 3x + C$, where C is some constant. But if $f(0) = 4$, then that means:

   $$4 = f(0) = (0)^2 - 3(0) + C, \text{ so } C = 4.$$

   Therefore:

   $$f(x) = x^2 - 3x + 4$$

2. If the derivative of our function is $0.6e^{3t}$, then our function is an antiderivative of $0.6e^{3t}$. By material in the previous part, our function has the form $0.2e^{3t} + C$. If we substitute $t = 0$ into this expression, the answer is supposed to be 5.2. Therefore:

   $$5.2 = .2e^{3(0)} + C$$
   $$= .2 + C$$

   Therefore, $C = 5$, and the function we want is $0.2e^{3t} + 5$.

3. The indefinite integral of $2 \sin x$ is $-2 \cos x + C$. Since $g(\pi) = 0$, we have

   $$-2 \cos \pi + C = 0$$
   $$-2(-1) + C = 0$$

   Hence $C = -2$, and $g(x) = -2 \cos x - 2$.

   Finally, $g\left(\frac{2\pi}{3}\right) = -2\left(-\frac{1}{2}\right) - 2 = -1$.

Antiderivatives. Exercise 2. Finding the Constant.

1. $f'(x) = -3$, $f(-1) = 4$

2. $f'(x) = e^x$, $f(0) = 0$

3. $f'(x) = \frac{4}{x} + 2$, $f(1) = 0$

4. $f'(x) = 3\sec^2 x - x$, $f(2) = -8$

5. $f'(x) = \frac{3}{4}x + 7$, $f(-8) = 12$

6. $f'(x) = .01x$, $f(100) = 17$

7. $f'(x) = .01x^2$, $f(100) = 17$

8. $f'(x) = .01(x^2 - x)$, $f(100) = 17$

9. $f'(x) = \frac{1}{x^2+1}$, $f(0) = 2$

10. $f'(x) = e^{2x-2} + 3x$, $f(2) = 4$

Part 3 Integration By Parts

Integration by parts is a technique used to integrate a function which is a product of two other functions. Integration by parts, however, is not a product rule in the sense that we are able to express the antiderivative of the product function in terms of the antiderivatives of the two factors. In fact, as mentioned earlier, THERE IS NO SUCH RULE. What integration by parts does is to trade in one integral for a second (hopefully easier) integral.

The basic formula for integration by parts says:

$$\int fg'\, dx = fg - \int f'g\, dx$$

(You can verify the formula by starting with the product formula for differentiation $(fg)' = fg' + f'g$, and then integrating both sides, remembering that $\int (fg)'\, dx = fg$.)

The most difficult step in using the integration by parts formula is choosing which factor is going to be f, and which is going to be g'. Here are a few ideas to keep in mind:

1. The product fg' must be the entire function inside the integral sign; everything in that function must be included in either f or g'.

2. The formula involves g, which is an antiderivative of g'. Therefore, whatever we choose for g', we must be able to find an antiderivative.

3. In <u>most</u> cases (some exceptions will be noted in the examples below), the integral $\int f'g\, dx$ should be easier to antidifferentiate than the original $\int fg'\, dx$.

Otherwise the right-hand side of the formula won't be any easier to deal with than the original problem.

Frequently, a good candidate for f is the function "x" itself. The advantage in that case is that $f' = 1$, so that the new integral will be just $\int g \, dx$.

Example:

Find $\int x \sin x \, dx$.

SOLUTION:

Using the hint above, we choose $f(x) = x$, so that $g'(x)$ has to be $\sin x$. It's a good idea to arrange f, g, f' and g' in the same kind of 2x2 array we used for various differentiation rules earlier:

$$f = x \qquad\qquad f' =$$
$$g = \qquad\qquad g' = \sin x$$

Now we need to fill in the blanks for f' and g. f' is easy, since it's the derivative of x, which is 1. To fill in g, we need an antiderivative for $g' = \sin x$. We could use any function of the form $-\cos x + C$, but life will be easiest with $C = 0$. So we fill in our 2x2 arrangement this way:

$$f = x \qquad\qquad f' = 1$$
$$g = -\cos x \qquad\qquad g' = \sin x$$

The integration by parts formula,

$$\int fg' \, dx = fg - \int f'g \, dx,$$

will give us, after the correct substitutions:

$$\int x \sin x \, dx = -x \cos x - \int (1)(-\cos x)dx$$
$$= -x \cos x - \int -\cos x \, dx$$
$$= -x \cos x - (-\sin x) + C$$
$$= -x \cos x + \sin x + C$$

If we use the differentiation rules from Volume 1 to find the derivative of $-x \cos x + \sin x + C$, we will find that we get $x \sin x$, just as we should.

Sometimes ln x is an even better choice for f than x itself.

That's because the derivative of ln x is $\frac{1}{x}$, which combines with other powers of x to make a function simpler than the original.

Example:

Find $\int \left(x^3 - 6x^2 + 2\right) \ln x \, dx$.

SOLUTION:

Following the hint above, we let $f = \ln x$, which forces g' to be $x^3 - 6x^2 + 2$. After we differentiate f to get f', and antidifferentiate g' to get g, our **2x2** array looks like this:

$$f = \ln x \qquad\qquad f' = \frac{1}{x}$$

$$g = \frac{x^4}{4} - 2x^3 + 2x \qquad\qquad g' = x^3 - 6x^2 + 2$$

Substituting into the formula for integration by parts, we get:

$$\int \left(x^3 - 6x^2 + 2\right)\ln x \, dx \;=\; \left(\frac{x^4}{4} - 2x^3 + 2x\right)\ln x - \int \left(\frac{1}{x}\right)\left(\frac{x^4}{4} - 2x^3 + 2x\right)dx$$

$$= \left(\frac{x^4}{4} - 2x^3 + 2x\right)\ln x - \int \left(\frac{x^3}{4} - 2x^2 + 2\right)dx$$

$$= \left(\frac{x^4}{4} - 2x^3 + 2x\right)\ln x - \left(\frac{x^4}{16} - \frac{2x^3}{3} + 2x\right) + C$$

$$= \left(\frac{x^4}{4} - 2x^3 + 2x\right)\ln x - \frac{x^4}{16} + \frac{2x^3}{3} - 2x + C$$

In some problems, we may still have a difficult integral after using the integration by parts formula once, but repeating the process will result in an integral which we can handle.

Example:

Find $\int x^2 \sin x \, dx$.

SOLUTION:

This problem is identical to the first example except that we have an x^2 instead of an x. Using an almost identical approach as in the first example, we choose $f = x^2$, so that g' is once again $\sin x$. After differentiating f and antidifferentiating g', our 2x2 array looks like this:

$$f = x^2 \qquad\qquad f' = 2x$$

$$g = -\cos x \qquad\qquad g' = \sin x$$

10

Now the integration by parts formula gives us:

$$\int x^2 \sin x \, dx = -x^2 \cos x - \int (-2x \cos x) dx$$

$$= -x^2 \cos x + \int 2x \cos x \, dx$$

(It is worth noting here that the integration by parts formula often produces a dizzying number of minus signs. We can reduce the likelihood of mistakes by canceling the minus signs whenever we can.)

Now the integral on the right-hand side doesn't look much easier than the original. However, we can invoke the integration by parts formula again, with f = 2x, and g′ = cos x.

$$f_1 = 2x \qquad\qquad f_1' = 2$$

$$g_1 = \sin x \qquad\qquad g_1' = \cos x$$

So now the integral on the right hand side of the equation above can be replaced by:

$$2x \sin x - \int 2 \sin x \, dx$$

Putting it all together, we have:

$$\int x^2 \sin x \, dx = -x^2 \cos x + 2x \sin x - \int 2 \sin x \, dx$$

$$= -x^2 \cos x + 2x \sin x - 2(-\cos x) + C$$

$$= -x^2 \cos x + 2x \sin x + 2 \cos x + C$$

Sometimes the function to be integrated doesn't seem to be a product of two other functions at all. But any function can be expressed as the product of 1 times itself. In other words, for any integral $\int f(x) dx$, we can let f = f(x), and g′ = 1. This idea may seem to complicate matters rather than simplify them, but there are some problems in which this approach gets results. The single most important case, which is worth memorizing, is the example below.

Example:

Find $\int \ln x \, dx$.

SOLUTION:

Conquering our doubts, we use integration by parts with f = ln x, and g′ = 1:

$$f = \ln x \qquad\qquad f' = \frac{1}{x}$$

$$g = x \qquad\qquad g' = 1$$

11

Now the new integral, $\int f'g\,dx$, on the right-hand side of the integration by parts formula, will be $\int\left(\frac{1}{x}\right)x\,dx$, or just $\int 1\,dx$. The entire formula gives us:

$$\int \ln x\ dx = x \ln x - \int x\left(\frac{1}{x}\right)dx$$

$$= x \ln x - \int 1\,dx$$

$$= x \ln x - x + C$$

The result of the previous example is important enough to state as a separate formula:

$$\boxed{\int \ln x\ dx = x \ln x - x + C}$$

Sometimes, applying the integration by parts method twice will result in an equation which contains more than one occurrence of the original integral, but no other integrals. The equation can then be solved using the original integral as the unknown.

Example:

Find $\int \sin(\ln x)dx$.

SOLUTION:

The function $\sin(\ln x)$ is not a product of two separate functions, so the only way to use integration by parts is to proceed as in the previous example, and let $f = \sin(\ln x)$, and $g' = 1$. Then our setup looks like this:

$$f = \sin(\ln x) \qquad\qquad f' = \frac{1}{x}(\cos(\ln x))$$

$$g = x \qquad\qquad g' = 1$$

(f' was calculated with the help of the chain rule).

Now the formula gives us:

$$\int \sin(\ln x)dx = x \sin(\ln x) - \int x\left(\frac{1}{x}\right)(\cos(\ln x))\,dx$$

$$\int \sin(\ln x)dx = x \sin(\ln x) - \int \cos(\ln x)dx \qquad \text{(Equation A)}$$

Now the new integral, $\int \cos(\ln x)dx$, does not seem any easier than the original. But we shall stubbornly continue, and try to integrate $\int \cos(\ln x)dx$ by using integration by parts again. We use $f = \cos(\ln x)$ and $g' = 1$:

$$f = \cos(\ln x) \qquad\qquad f' = \frac{1}{x}(-\sin(\ln x))$$

$$g = x \qquad\qquad g' = 1$$

Which gives us the equation:

$$\int \cos(\ln x)\,dx = x\cos(\ln x) - \int x\left(\frac{1}{x}\right)(-\sin(\ln x))\,dx$$

$$= x\cos(\ln x) - \int -\sin(\ln x)\,dx$$

$$= x\cos(\ln x) + \int \sin(\ln x)\,dx.$$

Now we can substitute for $\int \cos(\ln x)\,dx$ in "Equation A" above:

$$\int \sin(\ln x)\,dx = x\sin(\ln x) - \int \cos(\ln x)\,dx$$

$$= x\sin(\ln x) - \left(x\cos(\ln x) + \int \sin(\ln x)\,dx\right)$$

So we have:

$$\int \sin(\ln x)\,dx = x\sin(\ln x) - x\cos(\ln x) - \int \sin(\ln x)\,dx.$$

Now $\int \sin(\ln x)\,dx$ occurs twice in the equation, so we can treat the occurrences as "like terms". We therefore add $\int \sin(\ln x)$ to both sides of the equation:

$$2\left(\int \sin(\ln x)\,dx\right) = x\sin(\ln x) - x\cos(\ln x).$$

So, dividing both sides by 2, we get our answer:

$$\sin(\ln x)\,dx = \frac{1}{2}\left(x\sin(\ln x) - x\cos(\ln x)\right) + C$$

FINAL WARNING

Unlike the product rule for differentiation, the integration by parts procedure gives no guarantee of an answer. There are many functions which are expressed as the product of two or more other functions, for which an antiderivative <u>cannot</u> be found by using integration by parts. When we are *differentiating* a function, we can always decide for sure exactly what rule to use by determining the basic form of the function (product, quotient, etc.). But when integrating, we often have to flounder around, trying one idea and then another, until we find something that works.

Antiderivatives. Ingegration by Parts. Exercise 3.

In problems 1-12, find the indefinite integral of each function.

1. $\frac{x \sin x}{4}$

7. $\cos\left(\ln(x^3)\right)$

2. xe^{-x}

8. $e^{-3x} \sin x$

3. $e^{2x} \cos x$

9. $\ln\left(\frac{5x^2}{3}\right)$

4. $(3x - 1)\cos x$

10. $x^2 e^{3x}$

5. $2x \ln x$

11. $\cos^2 x$ (Hint : Use $\sin^2 x + \cos^2 x = 1$ at critical time.)

6. $\ln\left(\frac{2}{x}\right)$

12. $t \cos t \sin t$

13. Use problem 11 to develop a formula for $\int \cos^{2n} x \, dx$ in terms of $\int \cos^{2n-2} x \, dx$.

Part 4 Integration By Substitution

Integration by substitution is another integration technique which can sometimes transform a complicated integral into a simpler one. The bare-bones formula for integration by substitution is best expressed in terms of the " $\frac{d}{dx}$ " notation for the derivative:

$$\int\left(f(u)\frac{du}{dx}\right)dx = \int f(u)du$$

The formula requires some explanation. To integrate using substitution, we look for an undesirably complicated expression in the function, *whose derivative is a factor of the function*. The "undesirably complicated expression" will be our choice for "u". The derivative of the undesirably complicated expression, along with the "dx", will be replaced by "du". After the substitutions, we hope to have a simpler function than we started with, expressed in terms of u instead of x. In fact, every occurrence of x in the original integral will have to disappear, to be replaced by something involving u, in order for this procedure to work.

Example:

Find $\int 2x\, e^{x^2}\, dx$.

SOLUTION:

We know how to antidifferentiate e^x, but unfortunately the exponent in this example is more complicated. If we could replace the x^2 exponent with a single letter, we would be happier. Since the derivative of x^2 is $2x$, and since $2x$ is a factor of the function, we can do exactly what we want. We set up the substitutions as follows:

$$u = x^2$$

$$\frac{du}{dx} = 2x$$

Then, multiplying both sides by dx, we get

$$du = 2x\, dx$$

In order to clarify the procedure, we now rewrite the integral so that the 2x and the dx are next to each other:

$$\int e^{x^2}\, 2x\, dx$$

(We're allowed to do this because order doesn't make any difference when we multiply.)

Now, according to the substitutions we decided upon earlier, we replace the e^{x^2} with e^u, and replace 2x dx with du. The new integral is:

$$\int e^u du$$

We know that the antiderivative of e^u is e^u. So our answer will be $e^u + C$, except that we are obligated to express our answer in terms of x instead of u. Since we already know that $u = x^2$, that requirement is no hardship. We simply replace the u with x^2, and the answer is

$$e^{x^2} + C.$$

(As in all of our antidifferentiation examples, the reader should differentiate the answer, and expect to get the original function which we were trying to integrate.)

Once we choose an expression in x which we would like to replace with the single letter u, we don't really have to have the exact derivative of the expression as a factor of the integral. Any constant multiple of the derivative will do, since constant factors can always be factored out of the integral.

Example:

(a.) Find $\int \dfrac{3x^2}{\sqrt{x^3+14}}\,dx$

(b.) Find $\int \dfrac{x^2}{\sqrt{x^3+14}}\,dx$

SOLUTIONS:

(a) This integral would be much easier if we had just a single letter u under the radical on the bottom. We can do that, because the derivative of $x^3 + 14$ is $3x^2$, and $3x^2$ is a factor of the integral. Our substitutions are:

$$u = x^3 + 14$$

$du = 3x^2 dx$ (We usually go straight to an equation in this form instead of writing " $\frac{du}{dx} = 3x$ " and then multiplying both sides by dx.)

Replacing $x^3 + 14$ with u, and $3x^2$ dx with du, our new integral is:

$$\int \frac{1}{\sqrt{u}}\,du$$

NOTE that the only thing replaced by u was the expression $x^3 + 14$ itself. We did nothing to rid ourselves of the fraction or of the radical, so they stay where they are. The integral can now be rewritten in the more familiar form:

$$\int u^{-\frac{1}{2}}\,du$$

So the antiderivative is $\dfrac{u^{\frac{1}{2}}}{\frac{1}{2}} + C$, or $2\sqrt{u} + C$.

After replacing the u with $x^3 + 14$, we get the final answer:

$$2\sqrt{x^3 + 14} + C.$$

(b) This one is almost exactly like part (a). The difference is that the numerator of the fraction is x^2 instead of $3x^2$. This difference may appear to cause a big problem, but it doesn't. We still want to replace the $x^3 + 14$ with the single letter u, which means we need $3x^2$, the derivative of $x^3 + 14$, to be a factor of the function in order to complete the process. But x^2 (instead of $3x^2$) is close enough, as we shall see:

$$u = x^3 + 14$$

$$du = 3x^2 dx$$

Now, we don't have a $3x^2\,dx$ in the integral. But we do have $x^2\,dx$. So we manipulate the equation above so that $x^2\,dx$ appears on one side. This isn't hard, of course; we just multiply both sides of the equation by $\frac{1}{3}$, and we get:

$$\tfrac{1}{3}du = x^2 dx.$$

The appropriate substitutions in the original integral now result in:

$$\int \frac{1}{\sqrt{u}}\left(\tfrac{1}{3}\right)du$$

Of course, the "$\frac{1}{3}$" does not disturb us in the least, since we can always pull a constant factor right out of the integral and put it in front:

$$\int \frac{1}{\sqrt{u}}\left(\tfrac{1}{3}\right)du = \tfrac{1}{3}\int \frac{1}{\sqrt{u}}\,du = \tfrac{1}{3}\left(2\sqrt{u}\right)+C = \tfrac{2}{3}\sqrt{x^3+14}\;+C.$$

The last example might give the false impression that substitution can be used to simplify any integral at all. To cure that misunderstanding, we show two cases in which substitution cannot be used.

Non-examples:

(a) Find $\displaystyle\int \frac{1}{3x^2\sqrt{x^3+14}}\,dx$

(b) Find $\displaystyle\int \frac{3x^2 e^x}{\sqrt{x^3+14}}\,dx$

NON-SOLUTIONS:

a) We would like to substitute a single letter for the expression $x^3 + 14$. Since the derivative of $x^3 + 14$ is $3x^2$, and since there is a $3x^2$ in the denominator of the function, we might think that we can make the substitution we want. If we try that substitution, however, we get the following:

$$u = x^3 + 14$$

$$du = 3x^2 dx$$

BUT there is no $3x^2\,dx$ in the original function! What we <u>do</u> have is:

$$\int \frac{1}{\sqrt{x^3+14}}\left(\frac{1}{3x^2}\,dx\right)$$

And there is no way to convert the integral to the one we want.

b) If we choose to substitute $u = x^3 + 14$ in this case, we really do have the du we want:

$$u = x^3 + 14$$

$$du = 3x^2 dx$$

However, after making those substitutions, the integral would look like this:

$$\int \frac{e^x}{\sqrt{u}} du$$

It is impossible to calculate this integral, because it mixes x's and u's. We can antidifferentiate only when the entire expression is in terms of u, or the entire expression is in terms of x. We cannot pull the "e^x" out of the integral, the way we did with the "$\frac{1}{3}$" in a previous example, because e^x is not a constant. Therefore, we are out of luck.

If we want to substitute u for a <u>linear</u> function of x, we can <u>always</u> do it, because du will then be just a constant times dx. This observation is helpful in several different kinds of problems.

Examples:

(a) $\int \frac{2x}{3x-7} dx$

(b) $\int [\sec(5x + 1)][\tan(5x + 1)] dx$

SOLUTIONS:

a) Notice that if the fraction were turned upside down, so that the denominator were 2x, we could break the integral into the sum of two functions $\int \frac{3x}{2x}$ and $\int \frac{-7}{2x} dx$ which can easily be integrated separately. What the substitution procedure allows us to do is to transform the denominator into a single term. We let:

$$u = 3x - 7$$

so that $du = 3\ dx$,
  and $\frac{1}{3} du = dx$.

But what about the 2x in the numerator? We can solve $u = 3x - 7$ for x, which gives us:

$$x = \frac{1}{3}(u + 7)$$

therefore $2x = \frac{2}{3}(u + 7)$.

18

Gathering it all together, we have:

Old	New
3x - 7	u
2x	$\frac{2}{3}(u + 7)$
dx	$\frac{1}{3}du$

The new integral is:

$$\int \frac{\frac{2}{3}(u+7)}{u}\left(\frac{1}{3}du\right) = \frac{2}{9}\int \frac{u+7}{u}du$$

And from here, we work out the answer:

$$\frac{2}{9}\int \frac{u+7}{u}du = \frac{2}{9}\left(\int \frac{u}{u}du + \int \frac{7}{u}du\right) = \frac{2}{9}\left(\int 1 du + \int 7u^{-1}du\right)$$

$$= \frac{2}{9}\left(u + 7\ln|u| + C\right)$$

$$= \frac{2}{9}\left(3x - 7 + 7\ln|3x - 7|\right) + C.$$

b) Here we use u = 5x + 1, so that du = 5 dx. That means that $\frac{1}{5}du = dx$. The expression 5x + 1 occurs twice in the integral, and we will replace the expression with the letter u both times:

$$\int \left[\sec(5x + 1)\right]\left[\tan(5x + 1)\right]dx = \int \sec u \tan u\left(\frac{1}{5}du\right)$$

$$= \frac{1}{5}\int \sec u \tan u \, du = \frac{1}{5}\sec u + C$$

$$= \frac{1}{5}\sec(5x + 1) + C.$$

There are many cases in which integration by substitution can be combined with one or more trigonometric identities in order to solve a problem.

Example:

Find $\int \cos^3 x \, dx$.

SOLUTION:

The trick here is to realize two things:

(1) cosine is the derivative of the sine
(2) any even power of cosines can be converted to an expression involving sines by the use of the identity $\sin^2 x + \cos^2 x = 1$

19

As a first step, we will rewrite the integral this way:

$$\int \cos^2 x \cos x \, dx$$

Now we can replace $\cos^2 x$ with $(1 - \sin^2 x)$, by using the trigonometric identity mentioned above:

$$\int \left(1 - \sin^2 x\right) \cos x \, dx$$

Finally we use the substitution $u = \sin x$, which gives us:

$$u = \sin x$$

$$du = \cos x \, dx$$

Those substitutions result in a new integral:

$$\int \left(1 - u^2\right) du$$

which we can see works out to:

$$u - \frac{u^3}{3} + C$$

$$= \sin x - \frac{\sin^3 x}{3} + C$$

Sometimes the derivative of "u" has more than one term, which will not discourage us in the least.

Example:

Find $\int \left(e^{3x} - \frac{1}{3x}\right) \cos\left(e^{3x} - \ln^x\right)$.

SOLUTION:

This is much easier than it looks. We use:

$$u = e^{3x} - \ln x$$

$$du = 3e^{3x} - \frac{1}{x}, \text{ so that}$$

$$\tfrac{1}{3} du = \tfrac{1}{3}\left(3e^{3x} - \frac{1}{x}\right) = \left(e^{3x} - \frac{1}{3x}\right) dx$$

After which the problem can be solved simply:

$$\int \cos u \left(\tfrac{1}{3} du\right) = \tfrac{1}{3} \int \cos u \, du$$

$$= \tfrac{1}{3} \sin u + C = \tfrac{1}{3} \sin\left(e^{3x} - \ln x\right) + C$$

Antiderivatives. Integration and Substitution. Exercise 4.

In Problems 1-20, find the indefinite integral.

1. $\int \frac{2x-3}{x^2-3x+5} dx$

11. $\int \frac{e^{2t}+4t}{\left(\sqrt{e^{2t}+4t^2}\right)^3} dt$

2. $\int e^x \cos\left(e^x\right) dx$

12. $\int \frac{\sec^2(\ln x)}{x} dx$

3. $\int \frac{-\cos x}{e^{-\sin x}} dx$

13. $\int \frac{(\cos(\ln x))(\sin(\ln x))}{x} dx$

4. $\int (46x+23)\left(x^2+x-8\right)^{45} dx$

14. $\int \frac{2\ln x \, \sin\left[(\ln x)^2\right]}{x} dx$

5. $\int 2\sin^2(2x+1)\cos(2x+1) dx$

15. $\int 2\ln(3x-2) dx$

6. $\int \frac{\sec^2 x}{\tan x} dx$

16. $\int \frac{\tan x \, \sec^2 x}{e^{\tan^2 x}} dx$

7. $\int \frac{\sec^2 3x}{\tan 3x} dx$

17. $\int e^{2x} \sec^2\left(e^{2x}\right) dx$

8. $\int \frac{x+2}{x+1} dx$

18. $\int \left(r^2-r\right)\left(\sin\left(2r^3-3r^2+4\right)-e^{2r^3-3r^2+4}\right) dr$

9. $\int \frac{x^2+2}{x+1} dx$

19. $\int \sin^3 x \, dx$

10. $\int \frac{2x-3}{2\sqrt{x^2-3x+8}} dx$

20. $\int 3x^2 \sqrt{4-5x} \, dx$

21. Let $f'(x) = (16x+20)(2x^2+5x-1)^3$, and let $f(-3) = 11$. Find $f(x)$.

22. Let $f'(x) = \cos x \, e^{\sin x}$, and let $f\left(\frac{\pi}{6}\right) = 0$. Find $f(x)$.

23. Use an appropriate substitution to find a formula for $\int (ax+b)^n dx$, where
    a, b, and n are constants with $n \neq -1$.

24. Use the substitution $u = \frac{x}{a}$ to find $\int \frac{1}{\sqrt{a^2-x^x}} dx$.

25. Express tan x in terms of sin x and cos x to find $\int \tan x \, dx$.

26. Find $\int \cot x \, dx$.

Parts, Substitution, Both, or Neither?

An integration problem does not come with a sign hanging around its neck announcing "This is an Integration by Parts Problem" or "This is an Integration by Substitution Problem". Some integration problems can't be solved by either method, and some problems need a combination of the two. Identifying a problem as a likely candidate for integration by parts or for substitution is partly a matter of experience. However, there are a few rules of thumb.

1. Try first to spot a possible substitution. The tip-off is the presence of an expression, along with the derivative of that same expression, in the function to be integrated. Remember, as stated in the part on integration by substitution, that the substitutions must account for every occurrence of x (or the original variable, if it's something other than x) in the original integral, including the dx.

2. If no substitution seems likely to work, examine the possibility of integration by parts. Integration by parts is a particularly good bet if one of the factors of the function is either x itself, or ln x. If one of the factors is x to a positive integer power, then several successive applications of integration by parts may work. If the function to be integrated is not expressed as a product, we can always express it as fg' where g' is the constant "1" (see the example in Part 3 which calculates $\int \ln x \, dx$).

3. If it appears that the integral can be simplified by a substitution or a factorization for the integration by parts formula, then DO IT. Even if you can't foresee how to finish the problem, a look at the new, simplified integral might give you further ideas.

Example:

Find $\int x^3 e^{x^2} dx$.

SOLUTION:

First Solution:

If the function were $x\, e^{x^2}$ instead of $x^3 e^{x^2}$, then we would be able to use a substitution with $u = x^2$. In that case, du would be 2x dx and everything would be accounted for.

However, the realization that $\int x\, e^{x^2} dx$ would be solvable by substitution gives us an idea. Suppose we use integration by parts, with $f = x^2$. Then g' will have to be the remainder of the original function, namely $x\, e^{x^2}$.

Setting up our matrix of f, f', g and g', we get :

$$f = x^2 \qquad\qquad f' = 2x$$

$$g = ? \qquad\qquad g' = x\, e^{x^2}$$

In order to get g, we find the antiderivative $\int x\, e^{x^2}\, dx$ by using substitution:

$$u = x^2$$

$$du = 2x\, dx$$

$$\tfrac{1}{2} du = x\, dx$$

After the substitutions, we are looking for $\tfrac{1}{2}\int e^u du$, which is $\tfrac{1}{2} e^u$ or $\tfrac{1}{2} e^{x^2}$. So we fill in the "g" blank in our 2x2 array with $\tfrac{1}{2} e^{x^2}$:

$$f = x^2 \qquad\qquad f' = 2x$$

$$g = \tfrac{1}{2} e^{x^2} \qquad\qquad g' = x\, e^{x^2}$$

The integration by parts formula now gives:

$$\tfrac{1}{2} x^2 e^{x^2} - \int x\, e^{x^2}\, dx$$

The integral $\int x\, e^{x^2}\, dx$ is exactly what we just calculated, (namely $\tfrac{1}{2} e^{x^2}$) so the final answer is:

$$\tfrac{1}{2} x^2\, e^{x^2} - \tfrac{1}{2} e^{x^2} + C$$

Second Solution:

We could have started with substitution, with $u = x^2$:

$$u = x$$
$$du = 2x\, dx$$
$$\tfrac{1}{2} du = x\, dx$$

This idea works because we can express the x factor as x^3 times x^2. The "x^2" will be replaced by a u, and the "x" will become part of the du:

$$\int x^3 e^{x^2}\, dx = \int x^2 x\, e^{x^2}\, dx = \int u\, e^u du$$

The expression on the right-hand side, $\frac{1}{2}\int u\,e^u\,du$, can be solved using integration by parts, with:

$$f = u \qquad\qquad f' = 1$$

$$g = e^u \qquad\qquad g' = e^u$$

The formula gives us:

$$\frac{1}{2}\left(u e^u - \int e^u\,du\right)$$

$$= \frac{1}{2}\left(u e^u - e^u\right) + C$$

$$= \frac{1}{2}\left(x^2 e^{x^2} - e^{x^2}\right) + C$$

which is the same answer we got in the first solution.

Don't be too quick to use substitution or parts if you don't need to. Some seemingly complicated problems can be solved by using trigonometric identities, or even simple algebra such as the laws of exponents:

Examples:

1. Find $\int\left[\left(e^x\right)^3 - \left(e^x\right)^2\right] e^x\,dx$.

2. Find $\int\dfrac{dx}{\csc x\left(1-\sin^2 x\right)}$.

SOLUTIONS:

1. This problem seems to cry out for the substitution $u = e^x$, and in fact that would work. But no substitution is necessary if we remember the rules of exponents:

$$\int\left((e^x)^3 - (e^x)^2\right)e^x\,dx = \int\left(e^{3x} - e^{2x}\right)e^x\,dx$$

$$= \int\left(e^{4x} - e^{3x}\right)dx = \frac{e^{4x}}{4} - \frac{e^{3x}}{3} + C.$$

2. This problem looks perfectly awful. But if we remember how to simplify trigonometric expressions, we will find that it is not as bad as it looks:

$$\int\frac{dx}{\csc x\left(1-\sin^2 x\right)} = \int\frac{dx}{\frac{1}{\sin x}\left(\cos^2 x\right)} = \int\frac{1}{\frac{\cos^2 x}{\sin x}}\,dx$$

$$= \int\frac{\sin x}{\cos^2 x}\,dx = \int\frac{1}{\cos x}\frac{\sin x}{\cos x}\,dx = \int\sec x\,\tan x\,dx$$

$$= \sec x + C.$$

Example:

Find $\int \arcsin x \, dx$.

SOLUTION:

There is no substitution in sight, and the arcsin x is not a product of two functions—unless we express arcsin x as fg' with f = arcsin x and g' = 1. So we try our only hope:

$$f = \arcsin x \qquad\qquad f' = \frac{1}{\sqrt{1-x^2}}$$

$$g = x \qquad\qquad g' = 1$$

Now the integration by parts formula says that our original integral is equal to:

$$x \arcsin x - \int \frac{x}{\sqrt{1-x^2}} dx.$$

We can solve the integral on the right-hand side with a substitution:

$$u = 1 - x^2$$

$$du = -2x \, dx$$

$$-\frac{1}{2} du = x \, dx$$

So that we have:

$$x \arcsin x - \left(-\frac{1}{2} \int \frac{1}{\sqrt{u}} du \right)$$

$$= x \arcsin x + \frac{1}{2} \int u^{-\frac{1}{2}} du$$

$$= x \arcsin x + \sqrt{u} + C$$

$$= x \arcsin x + \sqrt{1-x^2} + C.$$

We can also find integrals of other inverse trigonometric functions with this approach. Those problems are in the exercises.

Antiderivatives. Parts, Substitution, Both, or Neither? Exercise 5.

In problems 1-17, find the indefinite integral of the given function.

1. $\sec^2 x \, e^{\tan x}$

7. $\cos x \cos(\sin x)$

2. $\dfrac{e^x + 15x^2}{e^x + 5x^3}$

8. $e^{5x-1} \sin x$

3. $\dfrac{1}{x \ln x}$

9. $\sin x \cos(\cos x)$

4. $4xe^{3x}$

10. $\tan^{-1} x$

5. $6x^2 e^{3x}$

11. $\tan^{-1}\left(2 - \frac{3}{4}x\right)$ (Use answer to #10.)

6. $e^x e^{e^x}$

12. $\dfrac{1}{x + x(\ln x)^2}$

13. $\dfrac{1}{\sqrt{x^2 - 1}}$ (Hint : Let $u = x + \sqrt{x^2 - 1}$ and put the expression for du over a common

denominator before proceeding further.)

14. $\dfrac{\cos x - 3e^{3x} + 20x^4 - 8}{\sqrt{\sin x - e^{3x} + 4x^5 - 8x + 1}}$

15. $x \cos\left(5x^2 - 4\right) \sin\left(5x^2 - 4\right)$

16. $\cos^{-1} x$

17. $\sin 2x \cos 5x$

18. Find the same procedure as in #17 to come up with a formula for $\int \sin ax \cos bx \, dx$.

Part 6 Partial Fractions

The integration of rational functions, such as $\dfrac{-3x-26}{x^2 - x - 6}$, is often difficult. On the other hand, we can calculate an integral such as $\int \dfrac{7}{x-3} dx$ with the substitution $u = x - 3$, and we get the answer:

$$\int \frac{7}{x-3} dx = 7 \ln|x - 3| + C.$$

The method of partial fractions is a procedure for transforming a function such as $\dfrac{-3x-26}{x^2 - x - 6}$ into a sum of more easily-handled functions like $\dfrac{7}{x-3}$.

We begin by stating the theorem on which the partial fractions method is based. To understand the theorem, we need the following technical definitions:

rational function = a fraction with a polynomial on the top and a polynomial on the bottom.

degree of a polynomial = the largest power of x in the polynomial.

proper rational function = one where the degree of the numerator is less than the degree of the denominator (equal degrees aren't good enough).

improper rational function = one where the degree of the numerator is greater than or equal to the degree of the denominator.

linear factor = a polynomial of degree 1.

"distinct" linear factors = a set of factors, no two of which are the same, and no factor is a constant multiple of another (for example we can't have x - 5 as one factor and 10 - 2x as another).

Now we're ready for the theorem:

Suppose R is a proper rational function whose denominator can be factored into n distinct linear factors f_1, f_2,.....f_n. Then there are numbers A_1, A_2,.....A_n such that:

$$R = \frac{A_1}{f_1} + \frac{A_2}{f_2} + \ldots\ldots + \frac{A_n}{f_n}.$$

Example:

Suppose $R = \frac{-3x-26}{x^2-x-6}$. Then the denominator can be factored as (x + 2) (x - 3), and the original R can be expressed this way:

$$\frac{-3x-26}{x^2-x-6} = \frac{4}{x+2} - \frac{7}{x-3}.$$

(We can apply simple algebra to the right-hand side to see that the two expressions are equal.)

Therefore we can calculate the integral $\int \frac{-3x-26}{x^2-x-6}dx$ this way:

$$\int \frac{-3x-26}{x^2-x-6}dx = \int \frac{4}{x+2}\,dx - \int \frac{7}{x-3}dx$$

$$= 4\ln|x + 2| - 7\ln|x - 3| + C.$$

Of course, the example above skipped over the question, "How did we find the 4 and the -7?" We now show the procedure which leads to the discovery of those two numbers.

Example:

> Find numbers A and B such that $\frac{-3x-26}{x^2-x-6} = \frac{A}{x+2} + \frac{B}{x-3}$.
>
> SOLUTION:
>
> We already know (from the theorem stated previously) that the two numbers A and B exist. If we put the two fractions on the right-hand side of the equation over a common denominator, the equation becomes:
>
> $$\frac{-3x-26}{x^2-x-6} = \frac{A(x-3)+B(x+2)}{(x+2)(x-3)}.$$
>
> Now the denominators on both sides of the equation are equal. Therefore, the numerators will also have to be equal. So we have the equation:
>
> $$-3x - 26 = A(x - 3) + B(x + 2).$$
>
> This equation is different from the kind we usually deal with, in the following sense: We are claiming that the left and right hand sides are in fact *the same function of x*, which can happen only if the equation is true for <u>all</u> values of x! An equation of this kind is called an *identity*. (The standard trigonometric identities are examples of this kind of equation - they are true no matter what values are substituted for the variables.) Therefore, we can select any number we please, substitute that value for x, and then rewrite the equation in hopes of a solution. We notice that if we choose x = 3, the expression A(x - 3) will become zero, simplifying the equation:
>
> $$-3(3) - 26 = 0 + B(3 + 2)$$
>
> $$-35 = 5B$$
>
> $$B = -7$$
>
> Similarly, if we choose x = -2, then the expression B(x + 2) will become zero, and our equation will be:
>
> $$-3(-2) - 26 = A(-2 - 3) + 0$$
>
> $$-20 = -5A$$
>
> $$A = 4$$
>
> Therefore, A = 4, B = -7, and the resulting identity is:
>
> $$\frac{-3x-26}{x^2-x-6} = \frac{4}{x+2} - \frac{7}{x-3}.$$

Of course, sometimes A and B are themselves fractions, but that doesn't make the process much harder.

Eample:

Find $\int \frac{3x^2+2x-1}{3x^3-11x^2-20x}\,dx.$

SOLUTION:

We first factor the denominator (see **Straight Forward Pre-Calculus**):

$$3x^3 - 11x^2 - 20x = x(3x + 4)(x - 5)$$

Second, we set up the partial fractions identity:

$$\frac{3x^2+2x-1}{3x^3-11x^2-20x} = \frac{A}{x} + \frac{B}{3x+4} + \frac{C}{x-5}.$$

If we put the right-hand side over a common denominator, then we will get:

$$\frac{3x^2+2x-1}{3x^3-11x^2-20x} = \frac{A(x-5)(3x+4)+B(x)(x-5)+C(x)(3x+4)}{x(x-5)(3x+4)}.$$

As before, since the denominators on both sides are equal, the numerators must be equal:

$$3x^2 + 2x - 1 = A(x - 5)(3x + 4) + B(x)(x - 5) + C(x)(3x + 4).$$

Following in the footsteps of the previous example, we choose values for **x** which will make the equation easy to solve for A, B, and C:

$$x = 5 : 3(5^2) + 2(5) - 1 = A(0) + B(0) + C(5)(19)$$

$$95C = 84$$

$$C = \frac{84}{95}$$

$$x = 0: \quad A(-20) = -1$$

$$A = \frac{1}{20}$$

$$x = -\frac{3}{4} \quad B\left(\frac{76}{9}\right) = \frac{15}{9}$$

$$B = \frac{15}{76}$$

Therefore the original function can be rewritten as:

$$\frac{\frac{1}{20}}{x} + \frac{\frac{15}{76}}{3x+4} + \frac{\frac{84}{95}}{x-5} \quad \text{or} \quad \frac{1}{20x} + \frac{15}{76(3x+4)} + \frac{84}{95(x-5)}$$

Now we are ready to integrate:

$$\int \frac{3x^2+2x-1}{3x^3-11x^2-20x} = \int \frac{1}{20x}\,dx + \int \frac{15}{76(3x+4)}\,dx + \int \frac{84}{95(x-5)}$$

$$= \frac{1}{20}\ln|x| + \frac{5}{76}\ln|3x+4| + \frac{84}{95}|x-5| + C.$$

(The antiderivatives of $\frac{15}{76(3x+4)}$ and $\frac{84}{95(x-5)}$ were found with the help of the substitutions $u = 3x + 4$ and $u = x - 5$ respectively.)

If our function is an improper rational function (the numerator has degree greater than or equal to the degree of the denominator), then we can convert the function into the sum of a polynomial plus a proper rational function, by using polynomial division. If we divide the denominator g(x) into the numerator f(x), we get a quotient q(x) and a remainder r(x). Those functions are related by the identity:

$$\frac{f(x)}{g(x)} = q(x) + \frac{r(x)}{g(x)}.$$

(See **Straight Forward Pre-Calculus**, Chapter 4, Part 1 for a description of polynomial division). In this case the quotient q(x) will be a polynomial, and the rational function $\frac{r(x)}{g(x)}$ will be a *proper* rational function. Since polynomials are easy to integrate, the partial fractions method will enable us to calculate the entire integral.

Example:

Find $\int \frac{x^2+1}{x^2-16}\,dx.$

SOLUTION:

The function is an improper rational function since the degree of the numerator is the same as the degree of the denominator. We use polynomial division to divide $x^2 + 1$ by $x^2 - 16$. By so doing, we find

$$q(x) = 1$$
$$r(x) = 17$$

This gives us the identity:

$$\frac{x^2+1}{x^2-16} = 1 + \frac{17}{x^2-16}.$$

And therefore:

$$\int \frac{x^2+1}{x^2-16}\,dx = \int 1\,dx + \int \frac{17}{x^2-16}\,dx.$$

30

The integral, $\int 1\,dx$, is equal to x (+ C), and we use partial fractions to calculate $\int \frac{17}{x^2-16}\,dx$. Since the denominator factors as (x - 4)(x + 4), our equation is:

$$\frac{17}{x^2-16} = \frac{A}{x-4} + \frac{B}{x-4}.$$

Following the standard procedure, we get:

$$A(x + 4) + B(x - 4) = 17$$

x = -4:
$$B(-8) = 17$$
$$B = -\frac{17}{8}$$

x = 4:
$$A(8) = 17$$
$$A = \frac{17}{8}$$

So our original integral can now be written and calculated as follows:

$$\int \frac{x^2+1}{x^2-16}\,dx = \int 1\,dx + \int \frac{17}{8(x-4)}\,dx - \int \frac{17}{8(x+4)}\,dx$$

$$= x + \frac{17}{8}\ln|x - 4| - \frac{17}{8}\ln|x + 4| + C.$$

The partial fractions method can be extended to a somewhat more complicated situation than those which we have dealt with so far. Suppose we are still dealing with a proper rational function whose denominator factors into linear factors, but this time one or more of those linear factors occurs more than once. Then the partial fraction decomposition may include fractions of the form:

$$\frac{A_1}{(ax+b)} + \frac{A_1}{(ax+b)^2} + \dots + \frac{A_n}{(ax+b)^n}$$

where n = the number of occurrences of the factor (ax + b) in the denominator.

Example:

Find $\int \frac{4x^2-17x+31}{x^3+3x^2-9x+5}\,dx$.

SOLUTION:

The denominator factors into $(x - 1)^2 (x + 5)$. So according to the expanded procedure described above, the function must be decomposable as follows:

$$\frac{4x^2-17x+31}{x^3+3x^2-9x+5} = \frac{A}{x-1} + \frac{B}{(x-1)^2} + \frac{C}{x+5}.$$

(If there had been a factor of $(x-1)^4$ in the denominator, we would have had $\frac{D}{(x-1)^3}$ and $\frac{E}{(x-1)^4}$ on the right-hand side as well.)

If we put the three right-hand fractions over a common denominator, we will multiply A by $(x - 1)(x + 5)$, B by $(x + 5)$, and C by $(x - 1)^2$. Since this numerator must be equal to the numerator of the original fraction, we have this equation:

$$A(x-1)(x+5) + B(x+5) + C(x-1)^2 = 4x^2 - 17x + 31$$

Setting $x = 1$, we get:

$$A(0) + B(6) + C(0) = 4(1^2) - 17(1) + 31 = 18$$
$$6B = 18$$
$$B = 3$$

If we set $x = -5$, we get $C(-6)^2 = 216$, so $C = 6$.

1 and -5 are the only two numbers which make everything easy for us by causing some of the left-hand terms to be zero. But we still can choose any other value we want for x. Since we now have the values for B and C, we can calculate the value of A easily with $x = 0$:

$$A(-1)(5) + B(5) + C(-1)^2 = 31$$
$$-5A + (3)(5) + 6 = 31$$
$$-5A = 10$$
$$A = -2$$

Therefore the original fraction is equal to

$$\frac{-2}{x-1} + \frac{3}{(x-1)^2} + \frac{6}{x+5}$$

and the integral is easily calculated as

$$-2\ln|x - 1| - \frac{3}{x-1} + 6\ln|x + 5| + C$$

Even if the factorization of the denominator includes one factor which is a constant multiple of another, that still counts as a factor which occurs more than once.

Example:

Find $\int \frac{8x^2-31x-121}{22x^3+80x-4x^3-450}\,dx.$

SOLUTION:

In this case, the denominator factors as

$$22x^2 + 80x - 4x^3 - 450 = (x - 5)(10 - 2x)(2x + 9)$$

But we have to recognize that $10 - 2x = -2(x - 5)$, so that we can also express the denominator as

$$-2(x - 5)^2 (2x + 9)$$

Therefore we set up the partial fractions equation this way:

$$\frac{A}{x-5} + \frac{B}{(x-5)^2} + \frac{C}{(-2)(2x+9)} = \frac{8x^2-31x-121}{22x^2+80x-4x^3-450}$$

The -2 could have been placed in any one of the three denominators; the answers we get for A, B, and C will make everything come out right.)

Following our usual procedure:

$$A(x - 5)(-2)(2x + 9) + B(-2)(2x + 9) + C(x - 5)^2 = 8x^2 - 31x - 121$$

With x = 5, we have:

$$A(0) + B(-2)(19) + C(0) = 8(25) - 31(5) - 121$$

$$-38B = -76$$

$$B = 2$$

Using x = -4.5:

$$C(-9.5)^2 = 180.5$$

$$C = 2$$

Using x = 6:

$$A(1)(-2)(21) + B(-2)(21) + C(1) = -19$$

$$-42A - 42B + C = -19$$

$$-42A - 84 + 2 = -19$$

$$-42A = 63$$

$$A = -1.5 \quad \left(\text{or } -\frac{3}{2}\right)$$

Now we can solve the original problem:

$$\int \frac{8x^2-31x-121}{22x^2+80x-4x^3-450} dx$$

$$= \int \left(\frac{-3}{2(x-5)} + \frac{2}{(x-5)^2} + \frac{2}{(-2)(2x+9)} \right) dx$$

$$= -\int \frac{3}{2(x-5)} dx + \int \frac{2}{(x-5)^2} dx - \int \frac{1}{2x+9} dx$$

$$= -\frac{3}{2} \ln|x - 5| - \frac{2}{x-5} - \frac{1}{2} \ln|2x - 9| + C.$$

Antiderivatives. Partial Fractions. Exercise 6.

Find the indefinite integral in each case.

1. $\int \frac{5x-1}{x^2-1} dx$

2. $\int \frac{22-2x}{15x^2-15} dx$

3. $\int \frac{40-13x^2-66x}{4x^3+28x^2+40x} dx$

4. $\int \frac{5x^2+50x-10}{3x^3+21x^2+30x} dx$

5. $\int \frac{x^2-17x-30}{x^3-10x^2} dx$

6. $\int \frac{3x-30-x^2}{x^3-10x^2} dx$

7. $\int \frac{8x+13}{2x^2+4x+2} dx$

8. $\int \frac{9x^3-21x^2-122x-30}{3x^2-15x} dx$

9. $\int \frac{6x^5-6x^4-9x^3+15x^2-8x+8}{3x^3-3x^2} dx$

10. $\int \frac{30x^5-30x^4-45x^3-87x^2-17x+5}{15x^3-15x^2} dx$

11. $\int \frac{49x^3+37x^2+26x-232}{6x^4-102x^2+96} dx$

12. $\int \frac{539x-320x^2-224}{50x^3-80x^2+32x} dx$

13. $\int \frac{8x^3+8x^2-7x-6}{x^4+2x^3+x^2} dx$

14. $\int \frac{6x^3+11x^2+3x-3}{x^4+x^3} dx$

15. $\int \frac{1}{x^2-9x+14} dx$

16. $\int \frac{3}{x^2-16} dx$

Miscellaneous Integration Problems. Exercise 7.

This Part is just a collection of exercises. In each case, find the requested indefinite integral using any of the techniques introduced so far.

1. $\int \frac{e^{2x}+3e^x-5}{e^x} dx$

2. $\int (x-1)\sin x \, dx$

3. $\int \frac{3x^4-2\sqrt{x}+5x^2-3}{4x^2} dx$

4. $\int (\ln x)\left(5x^5 + 4x^4 - 3x^3\right) dx$

5. $\int \frac{6x^4-15x^3-33x^2+5x+11}{3x^3-9x-6} dx$

6. $\int x^2 \sin x \, dx$

7. $\int \frac{-15x^2-28x-19}{3x^3-9x-6} dx$

8. $\int x \arcsin x^2 \, dx$

9. $\int \frac{x^2+1}{x^2-3x+2} dx$

10. $\int (6x - 4)\cos\left(3x^2 - 4x\right)e^{\sin(3x^2-4x)} dx$

11. $\int \frac{x+1}{x^2-3x+2} dx$

12. $\int \frac{\cos x - \sec^2 x}{\sin x - \tan x} dx$

13. $\int \frac{1}{x^2-3x+2} dx$

14. $\int (3x + 1)\left(\sin(3x^2 + 2x + 1)\right)\cos^2\left(3x^2 + 2x + 1\right) dx$

15. $\int \frac{2x\left(x^2+3\right)}{\left(x^2+1\right)^2} dx$

16. $\int (3x + 1)\sin\left(3x^2 + 2x + 1\right) dx$

17. $\int 2x\left(x^2 - 3\right)^2 \sin\left(x^2 - 3\right) dx$

18. $\int \frac{-6}{1+(4-3x)^2} dx$

19. $\int \frac{x^2}{e^x} dx$

20. $\int \frac{\left(8x-\sec^2 x\right)e^{\left(4x^2-\tan x\right)}\cos\left(e^{4x^2-\tan x}\right)}{\sin\left(e^{4x^2-\tan x}\right)} dx$

Definite Ingegrals

If we want to calculate the area of a nice, symmetrical shape such as a circle, rectangle, or triangle, we have a simple geometric formula for doing so. However, we would like a more general method for calculating area. For example, suppose f(x) is a function such that f(x) ≥ 0 everywhere on the interval (-2,5). Then the graph of y = f(x) will be on or above the x-axis for the entire interval (-2,5). We would like to know how to calculate the area of the region A in the diagram below. The region A is bounded above by the graph of f(x), below by the x-axis, on the left by the vertical line x = -2, and on the right by the vertical line x = 5.

We will begin by looking at functions whose graph forms a familiar geometrical shape, so that we can calculate the desired area with formulas already known from elementary geometry.

Example:

Find the area of the region bounded on the left by x = -2, on the right by x = 5, below by the x-axis, and above by y = 3.

SOLUTION:

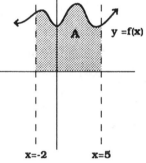

Notice that we can think of the upper boundary of this region as the graph of the constant function f(x) = 3. The region whose area we want to calculate is shown in the diagram.

Since the region is a rectangle of width 7 and height 3, the calculation is easy:

    A = 7 ·3 = 21

However, let us notice something else:

    g(x) = 3x is an antiderivative for the constant function f(x) = 3. The area, 21, is equal to:

        15 - (-6)
        = 3(5) - 3(-2)
        = g(5) - g(-2).

The last observation in the example above was no coincidence! We will show two more examples.

Examples:

1. Find the area between the x-axis and the graph of y = x, bounded on the left by the y-axis, and on the right by the vertical line x = 6.

2. Find the area between the x-axis and the graph of the function f(x) = 15 - 2x, from x = -4 on the left to x = 5 on the right.

SOLUTIONS:

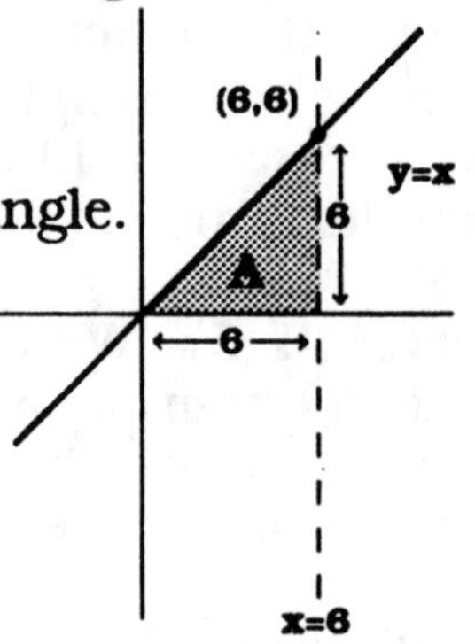

1. The area we need to compute is that of a right triangle. The formula for the area of a triangle is $A = \frac{1}{2}bh$, where b = length of the base, and h = height. In this case, both the length and the height are equal to 6, and so the area is:

$$\frac{1}{2} \cdot 6^2 = 18$$

Following the idea we used at the end of the previous example, notice that $g(x) = \frac{1}{2}x^2$ is an antiderivative for the function f(x) = x, and that:

$$18 = A = \frac{1}{2}(6)^2 - \frac{1}{2}(0)^2$$
$$= g(6) - g(0).$$

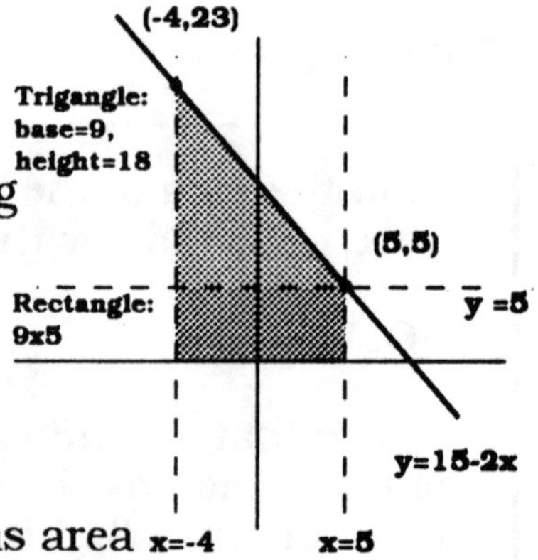

2. The region whose area we want is shown in the diagram. For purposes of calculating the area, we can divide the region into a rectangle and a triangle, as shown. (We could use the formula for the area of a right trapezoid instead, but most people don't remember that formula.)

The rectangle at the bottom of the region has area $9 \cdot 5 = 45$, and the area of the triangle is $\frac{1}{2}(9 \cdot 18) = 81$. Therefore the total area we want is 45 + 81 = 126.

Once again, we look at an antiderivative of 15 - 2x, g(x) = 15x - x². We calculate g(5) = 50, and g(-4) = -76.

So: Area = 126
          = 50 - (-76)
          = g(5) - g(-4).

The last step of each example above leads to the hope that an antiderivative may be of some value in calculating the area of a region bounded above by the graph of y = f(x). In fact this hope will be fulfilled by a theorem below. First, however, we introduce a mathematical symbol for the area of a region such as the ones we have been dealing with. The use of the integral symbol is justified by our discovery that antiderivatives can often be used to calculate the area of a region.

TEMPORARY DEFINITION:

$$\int_a^b f(x)dx = \begin{cases} \text{The area of the region bounded on the left by x = a,} \\ \text{on the right by x = b, below by the x-axis, and above} \\ \text{by the graph of y = f(x). The numbers a and b in this} \\ \text{symbol are called the \underline{limits of integration}.} \end{cases}$$

The symbol $\int_a^b f(x)dx$ is called the definite integral of f on the interval $[a, b]$.

Although the definition above is accurate as far as it goes, it is not a precise mathematical definition and will be replaced by a more mathematically rigorous definition in Part 3.

Examples:

The calculations in the first example of this Part show that $\int_{-2}^{5} 3dx = 21$.

The two problems in the second example show that $\int_0^6 x\,dx = 18$ and

that $\int_{-4}^{5}(15 - 2x)dx = 126$.

The definition we have just given makes several assumptions. For one thing, the definition makes sense only if a ≤ b. Otherwise, the region in question cannot be bounded on the left by x = a and on the right by x = b. Similarly, there is an assumption that f(x) ≥ 0 everywhere on the interval from $[a, b]$. Otherwise, the graph of y = f(x) would be below the x-axis for at least part of the interval [a,b]. That would make it impossible for the upper boundary of the region to be the graph y = f(x) and the lower boundary to be the x-axis. We will eliminate these two restrictions with the following conventions:

1. Any region lying below the x-axis will be assumed to have a negative area. The magnitude of the area will be the same as if the region were above the x-axis, except that it will be negative.

2. If b ‹ a, then $\int_a^b f(x)dx = -\int_b^a f(x)dx$. In other words, if the number at the top is smaller than the number at the bottom, we can switch the two numbers and then multiply the answer by -1.

EXAMPLES:

1. Find $\int_0^6 \left(\frac{1}{2}x - 3\right) dx$.

2. Find $\int_0^{12} \left(\frac{1}{2}x - 3\right) dx$.

3. Find $\int_6^0 \left(\frac{1}{2}x - 3\right) dx$.

SOLUTIONS:

The diagram below illustrates the situation for all three problems.

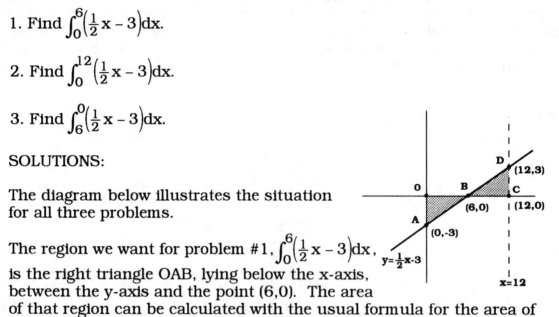

The region we want for problem #1, $\int_0^6 \left(\frac{1}{2}x - 3\right) dx$, is the right triangle OAB, lying below the x-axis, between the y-axis and the point (6,0). The area of that region can be calculated with the usual formula for the area of a triangle, and comes out to be $\frac{1}{2}(6)(3) = 9$. Since the region lies below the x-axis, however, the area is negative, and so our answer is -9.

For problem #2, the region is the triangle OAB which we used for problem #1, plus the triangle BCD above the x-axis, from the point (6,0) to the vertical line x = 12. It is easy to see that the triangles OAB and BCD are congruent and therefore have the same area. However, the area of the triangle OAB is negative 9, whereas triangle BCD is above the x-axis and therefore has an area of positive 9. So the total area is -9 + 9 = 0.

The region in problem #3 is exactly the same as for problem #1. The only difference is that we have switched the limits of integration, which has the effect of multiplying the area by -1. Since the answer to #1 was -9, the area we want for #3 is (positive) 9.

Now that the symbol $\int_a^b f(x)dx$ has a definition for cases in which f(x) is either positive or negative, and in which **a** can be either less than or greater than **b**, we are ready to state the

Fundamental Theorem of Calculus (First Version):

If f is continuous on the closed interval $[a, b]$, and if g is an antiderivative for f, then

$$\int_a^b f(x)dx = g(b) - g(a)$$

Examples:

Use the Fundamental Theorem of Calculus to calculate the areas in the three problems given in the previous example, namely:

1. Find $\int_0^6 \left(\frac{1}{2}x - 3\right)dx$.

2. Find $\int_0^{12} \left(\frac{1}{2}x - 3\right)dx$.

3. Find $\int_6^0 \left(\frac{1}{2}x - 3\right)dx$.

SOLUTIONS:

The function $g(x) = \frac{1}{4}x^2 - 3x$ is an antiderivative for $\frac{1}{2}x - 3$, so we can use $g(x)$ to calculate the areas according to the formula given by the Fundamental Theorem of Calculus:

1. $\int_0^6 \left(\frac{1}{2}x - 3\right)dx \quad = \quad g(6) - g(0)$
$$= -9 - 0$$
$$= -9.$$

2. $\int_0^{12} \left(\frac{1}{2}x - 3\right)dx \quad = \quad g(12) - g(0)$
$$= 0 - 0$$
$$= 0.$$

3. $\int_6^0 \left(\frac{1}{2}x - 3\right)dx \quad = \quad g(0) - g(6)$
$$= 0 - (-9)$$
$$= 9.$$

All three answers are the same as we calculated geometrically in the previous example.

What Happened to the "+ C"?

The general form for an antiderivative of a function has a "+ C" at the end. However, when calculating a definite integral, we always use the shortest and simplest antiderivative we can find. In other words, we assume C = 0. That's because no matter what value we assign to C, the "+ C" will drop out of the calculation of a definite integral. Therefore we might as well use the easiest possible C, which is almost always zero.

Example:

> Calculate $\int_2^6 3x^2 \, dx$ twice: first using an antiderivative with C = 0, and then using an antiderivative with C = -187.
>
> SOLUTION:
>
> The indefinite integral of $3x^2$ is x^3 + C. Using C = 0, we choose the antiderivative $g(x) = x^3$, and then:
>
> $$\int_2^6 3x^2 \, dx = g(6) - g(2)$$
> $$= 216 - 8$$
> $$= 208.$$
>
> If we choose C = -187, then we will be using the antiderivative $h(x) = x^3 - 187$, and so:
>
> $$\int_2^6 3x^2 \, dx = h(6) - h(2)$$
> $$= 29 - (-179)$$
> $$= 208.$$
>
> So the -187 made no difference at all.

For a more general demonstration, suppose that g is an antiderivative of f for which we chose C = 0, and then we let $g_2 = g_1 + C$ where C is some nonzero number. Then:

$$g_2 = g_1 + C$$

so that

$$g_2(b) - g_2(a) = (g_1(b) + C) - (g_1(a) + C)$$
$$= g_1(b) + C - g_1(a) - C$$
$$= g_1(b) - g_1(a).$$

Fundamental Theorem of Calculus (Second Version)

The second version of the Fundamental Theorem of Calculus involves a strange-looking function:

$$A(x) = \int_a^x f(t)dt \quad \text{(where a is some constant).}$$

The function A(x) requires some explanation. Imagine that the function f(t) is graphed on a t-y plane. Once we choose a value for a, the value of the function A(x) will be the area of the region in the t-y plane bounded by t = a, t = x, the t-axis, and the graph of y = f(t).

40

EXAMPLE:

Let $A(x) = \int_{\pi}^{x} \sin t \, dt$.   Find:

1. $A(2\pi)$,

2. $A(17)$.

3. $A(0)$

SOLUTIONS:

From the first version of the Fundamental Theorem of Calculus, we can calculate all three of these answers with -cos x, which is an anti-derivative for sin x.

1. $A(2) = \int_{\pi}^{x} \sin t \, dt$
    $= -\cos(2\pi) - (-\cos(\pi))$
    $= -1 - 1$
    $= -2$.

2. $A(17) = -\cos(17) - (-\cos(\pi))$
    $= .27516 - 1$
    $= -0.72484$.

3. $A(0) = -\cos(0) - (-\cos(\pi))$
    $= -1 - 1$
    $= -2$.

The second version of the Fundamental Theorem of Calculus makes a statement about the function A(x).

Fundamental Theorem of Calculus (Second Version)

Suppose f(x) is continuous on the interval. Then the function
$A(x) = \int_{a}^{x} f(t) \, dt$ is an antiderivative of f(x).

Remember that a function can be continuous without having a derivative. However, the second version of the Fundamental Theorem tells us that a continuous function must have an <u>anti</u>derivative.

Example:

f(x) = |x| is a continuous function which has no derivative at x = 0. However, we can find an antiderivative for |x| by defining

$$A(x) = \int_{0}^{x} |x| \, dt.$$

41

If we remember the definition of $|x|$:

$$|x| = \begin{cases} -x & x < 0 \\ x & x \geq 0. \end{cases}$$

Then we can see that if $x \geq 0$, then

$$\int_0^x |t|\, dt = \int_0^x t\, dt$$

$$= \tfrac{1}{2}x^2 - \tfrac{1}{2}0^2$$

$$= \tfrac{1}{2}x^2.$$

On the other hand, if $x < 0$, then

$$\int_0^x |t|\, dt = \int_0^x -t\, dt$$

$$= -\int_0^x t\, dt$$

$$= \int_x^0 t\, dt$$

$$= \tfrac{1}{2}0^2 - \tfrac{1}{2}x^2$$

$$= -\tfrac{1}{2}x^2$$

Putting the results together, we have:

$$A(x) = \begin{cases} -\tfrac{1}{2}x^2 & x < 0 \\ \tfrac{1}{2}x^2 & x \geq 0. \end{cases}$$

Note that A(x), as we defined it, is differentiable at $x = 0$ since the derivatives of both $\tfrac{1}{2}x^2$ and $-\tfrac{1}{2}x^2$ are both equal to 0 (which is $|0|$) at $x = 0$.

BIG-TIME WARNING:

Notice that both versions of the Fundamental Theorem of Calculus require the function being integrated to be continuous on the closed interval $[a, b]$. The methods in this section do not apply to integrals such as

$$\int_0^\pi \tan x\, dx \quad \text{or} \quad \int_0^4 \frac{1}{x^2}.$$

Definite Integrals. Fundamental Theorem of Calculus. Exercise 1.

In Problems 1-24, calculate the value of the definite integral.

1. $\int_0^1 x\,e^{4x}$

2. $\int_2^0 8(4x-3)^7\,dx$

3. $\int_0^{-2} x^2\,dx$

4. $\int_{-\pi}^{\frac{-3\pi}{2}} x\cos x\,dx$

5. $\int_3^2 \left(x-\frac{1}{3}\right)e^{3x^2-2x}$

6. $\int_{-1}^1 \cos\Theta\,d\Theta$

7. $\int_{-3}^{-1}\frac{-x-20}{x^2-16}\,dx$

8. $\int_1^4 \frac{3x-1}{3x^2-2x}\,dx$

9. $\int_3^{10}\frac{5}{\sqrt{x}}\,dx$

10. $\int_2^{-.5}\frac{3x}{(x+1)^2}$

11. $\int_\pi^{\frac{5\pi}{4}} \tan x\,\sec^2 x\,dx$

12. $\int_{-2}^0 e^{-3x}$

13. $\int_3^{-1}\frac{5-8x}{2x^2-7x-22}\,dx$

14. $\int_{0.1}^4 (\ln t)\left(t^2-4t\right)dt$

15. $\int_4^{0.1}\frac{4x^2-3x+2}{x}\,dx$

16. $\int_0^{-2}\frac{3x^2-30x+73}{3(x-5)^3}\,dx$

17. $\int_{-\pi}^{-3\pi}(x-2)\cos(x-2)dx$

18. $\int_{200}^{100}-8dy$

19. $\int_{-2}^{-1}\frac{5x^2+26x+36}{x^3+6x^2+9x}dx$

20. $\int_{-\pi}^{\pi} \sin x\,\sin 3x\,dx$

21. $\int_2^5 \frac{6x+3}{\sqrt{x^2+x+8}}\,dx$

22. $\int_{-1}^2 \frac{4x^2+25x+36}{x^2+5x+6}\,dx$

23. $\int_{-6}^{-3} x^2 e^x\,dx$

24. $\int_{-1}^2 -28(4x-3)^7\cos\left[(4x-3)^8\right]dx$

25. Suppose $f(x)=\int_0^x \sqrt{x^2-4x+19}$. Find $f'(3)$.

26. Let $f(3) = 12$ and $f(6) = 20$. Find $\int_6^3 f'(t)dt$.

Sigma Notation

Sometimes a mathematical formula involves a long sum, or a sum whose length can vary from one application to another. For example, we can get the average age of a group of people by adding all their ages together and then dividing by the number of people. This method works whether the group has 5 people or 500 people. Sigma notation provides a concise way of referring to the sum even before we know how many terms are in the sum.

If b is a positive integer, and if c_1, c_2, c_3,......c_b are numbers of any kind, then we define

$$\sum_{k=1}^{b} c_k \quad \text{to mean:} \quad c_1 + c_2 + c_3 + ...c_b.$$

The symbol $\sum$ is a Greek capital Sigma, which is used to stand for the word "sum." The "k = 1" at the bottom means that we start by substituting k = 1. For each term thereafter, we add 1 to the previous k and include c_k in the sum. The "b" at the top tells us where to stop: c_b is the last term of the sum.

Examples:

1. Suppose c_1 = -3, c_2 = -1, c_3 = 0, c_4 = -2, and c_5 = 55.

   Then $\sum_{k=1}^{5} c_k = -3 - 1 + 0 - 2 + 55 = 49,$

   and $\sum_{k=1}^{3} c_k = -3 - 1 + 0 = -4.$

2. Suppose $c_k = 2k - 1$ for all k.

   Then $\sum_{k=1}^{3} c_k = ((2 \cdot 1) - 1) + ((2 \cdot 2) - 1) + ((2 \cdot 3) - 1) = 1 + 3 + 5 = 9.$

   and $\sum_{k=1}^{1} c_k = (2 \cdot 1) - 1 = 1.$

3. Suppose $f(x) = .01e^{x^2}$, and suppose $c_k = f(k)$ for all k.

   Then $\sum_{k=1}^{4} c_k = .02718 + .54598 + 81.03084 + 88861.10521$

   $= 88942.70921.$

Often we use some algebraic expression involving k, instead of c_k, in the sigma notation: Examples 2 and 3 above could have been represented

$$\sum_{k=1}^{3}(2k-1) \text{ and } \sum_{k=1}^{4}.01e^{k^2} \text{ respectively.}$$

Although the sum described in sigma notation usually begins with k = 1, it is perfectly legal for the sum to begin at any integer at all.

EXAMPLES:

1. Represent the sum of all the even numbers from 20 through 50 in sigma notation.

2. Represent the sum of the squares of the first n integers in sigma notation.

SOLUTIONS:

1. We can restrict the sum to even numbers by using the expression 2k, where 2k is an integer. This problem then requires us to begin with k = 10 (so that the first "2k" will be 20) and finish with k = 25:

$$\sum_{k=10}^{25}2k.$$

2. The answer should be self-explanatory:

$$\sum_{k=1}^{n}k^2.$$

There are several rules for manipulating expressions in sigma notation to make the expressions easier to calculate with:

1. $\displaystyle\sum_{k=a}^{b}rc_k = r\left(\sum_{k=a}^{b}c_k\right)$ for any constant r.

2. $\displaystyle\sum_{k=a}^{b}(c_k + d_k) = \left(\sum_{k=a}^{b}c_k\right) + \left(\sum_{k=a}^{b}d_k\right).$

3. If $a \le n < b$, then

$$\sum_{k=a}^{b}c_k = \left(\sum_{k=a}^{n}c_k\right) + \left(\sum_{k=n+1}^{b}c_k\right).$$

The first of the rules above is simply the distributive law applied to a sum of arbitrary lengths. The second rule is a consequence of the commutativity of addition - it says that when we add, we can rearrange the terms of the sum in any order. The third rule just says that we can split the sum into a sum of the first n terms plus the sum of the last (b - n) terms.

Definite Integrals. Sigma Notation. Exercise 2.

In problems 1-8, find the indicated sum.

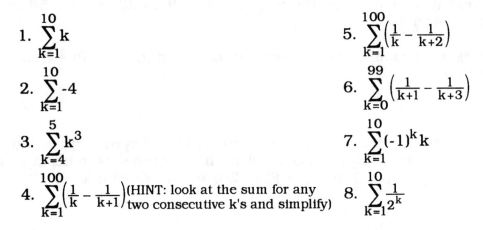

1. $\displaystyle\sum_{k=1}^{10} k$

2. $\displaystyle\sum_{k=1}^{10} -4$

3. $\displaystyle\sum_{k=4}^{5} k^3$

4. $\displaystyle\sum_{k=1}^{100} \left(\frac{1}{k} - \frac{1}{k+1}\right)$ (HINT: look at the sum for any two consecutive k's and simplify)

5. $\displaystyle\sum_{k=1}^{100} \left(\frac{1}{k} - \frac{1}{k+2}\right)$

6. $\displaystyle\sum_{k=0}^{99} \left(\frac{1}{k+1} - \frac{1}{k+3}\right)$

7. $\displaystyle\sum_{k=1}^{10} (-1)^k k$

8. $\displaystyle\sum_{k=1}^{10} \frac{1}{2^k}$

In problems 9-12, rewrite the sum in sigma notation.

9. $3 + 4 + 5 + ... + 1234.$

10. $4 + 6 + 8 + ... + 1234.$

11. $\frac{2}{3} + \frac{2}{9} + \frac{2}{27} + ... + \frac{2}{177147}.$

12. $\frac{2}{3} - \frac{4}{9} - \frac{8}{27} - \frac{16}{81} + ... + \frac{512}{19683} - \frac{1024}{59049}$ (NOTE : $1024 = 2^{10}$, $59049 = 3^{10}$.).

46

Our previous temporary definition of a definite integral suffers from the fact that we have no mathematically precise definition of the word "area." A square inch can easily be defined as the area of a square with each side one inch long. That definition can be expanded to include any rectangle, by defining the area to be the product of the length and the width. But a region bounded by irregular curves has no constant width or length - the dimensions vary from one point to another.

It is the limit idea in calculus which saves the day. Informally, the calculus idea of area is to overlay the region with a collection of rectangles. The sum total of the rectangular areas will not, perhaps, include the entire region. It also may be that some of the rectangles will stray outside the region. But as we use a larger and larger number of smaller and smaller rectangles, the collection of rectangles will do a better and better job of approximating the actual area of the region. This idea is similar to the observation that you can fill a jar more completely with sand than you can with marbles. Since grains of sand are comparatively tiny, they will pack together and leave much less dead air space than marbles will. Below we show a diagram in which the area under the graph from x = 0 to x = 5 has been approximated by 2 rectangles, and then another diagram in which the same area has been approximated by 5 rectangles.

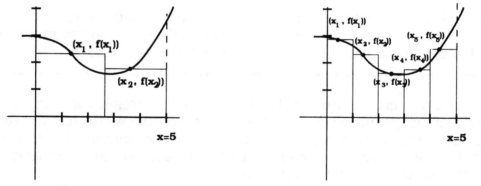

Notice that in both diagrams, the interval $[0,5]$ has been divided into equal subintervals. Each subinterval, along the x-axis, is used as the "floor" of a rectangle. The height of each rectangle is the height of the graph at some randomly chosen point in the subinterval. As we know, the "height" of the graph of f(x) at any point is the y-coordinate of the point. The y-coordinate, in turn, is the value of f(c), where c is the x-coordinate of the point. Therefore, in the diagrams above, the height of the "kth" rectangle is $f(x_K)$.

Our goal is to find the area of the region under a graph, from x = a to x = b. Using the rectangles above as approximations to the region itself, we can calculate the area of the kth rectangle as (d) ·(f(x)), where d = the width of each subinterval, and x_K = some randomly chosen value in the kth subinterval. If we add the areas of all the rectangles together, the formula is:

$$\sum_{k=1}^{n} d \cdot f(x_k) = d\left(\sum_{k=1}^{n} f(x_k)\right)$$

where n = the number of subintervals.

The sum defined above is called a **Riemann Sum** for f(x) over the interval $[a, b]$.

Several important comments about the Riemann sums:

1. If we want to divide the interval $[a, b]$ into n equal subintervals, then the width d of each subinterval can be calculated by the formula:

$$d = \frac{b-a}{n}.$$

   (NOTE: All the subintervals don't really have to have the same width. If we use a different width for each subinterval, then we would use the notation d_k for the width of the kth subinterval, and the sum formula would be:

$$\sum_{k=1}^{n} d_k \cdot f(x_k)$$

   However, for the sake of simplicity we will work on the assumption that we always divide interval $[a, b]$ up into subintervals which all have the same width.)

2. If $f(x_k)$ is negative, then the point $(x_k, f(x_k))$ will be below the x-axis. Hence, the kth rectangle will also lie below the x-axis. Therefore, this definition retains the property that the area of a region lying below the x-axis is negative.

3. The value of a Riemann sum depends greatly upon the choice of the points x_k. However, the definition below, along with the theorem mentioned after it, will show that the choice is not as important as it seems.

As we said earlier, the sum of the areas of the rectangles will approximate the area under the graph more and more closely as the width of each rectangle decreases (and the number of rectangles therefore increases). In fact, this observation leads us to the more mathematically precise definition of a definite integral, which was promised in Part 1.

Permanent Definition:

$$\int_a^b f(x)dx = \lim_{d \to 0}\left(\sum_{k=1}^{n} d \cdot f(x_k)\right)$$

where the interval $[a, b]$ is divided up into n equal subintervals of width d, and x_k is some number in the kth subinterval.

The following theorem is something of a surprise:

The limit used in the definition above exists whenever f(x) is continuous on $[a, b]$, and *the limit comes out the same regardless of the choices of the* x_k's.

Furthermore, <u>both versions of the Fundamental Theorem of Calculus are true</u> <u>when the definite integral is defined as above</u>.

Since $d = \frac{b-a}{n}$, d approaches zero as n approaches infinity.

Therefore, an alternate definition of the definite integral is:

$$\int_a^b f(x)dx = \lim_{n \to \infty} \left(\frac{b-a}{n} \sum_{k=1}^{n} f(x_k) \right)$$

The calculation of the limit of a Riemann sum is often difficult. However, we can sometimes get a rough approximation by partitioning the interval $[a,b]$ into a non-frightening number of subintervals, and choosing our x_k's according to whatever method seems most pleasant. There are three fairly obvious choices for x_k in the kth subinterval: the left-hand endpoint, the right-hand endpoint, and the midpoint.

Example:

Estimate the integral $\int_{-2}^{2} x^2 dx$ by dividing the interval $[-2,2]$ into 4 equal subintervals, and choosing:

     a. x_k to be the left-hand endpoint of kth subinterval

     b. x_k to be the right-hand endpoint of kth subinterval

     c. x_k to be the midpoint of kth subinterval.

SOLUTIONS:

The four equal subintervals will be:

$$[-2,-1]$$
$$[-1,0]$$
$$[0,1]$$
$$\text{and } [1,2]$$

The value of d will be $\frac{2-(-2)}{4} = 1$.

a. The left-hand endpoints of the four subintervals are -2, -1, 0, and 1. We have f(-2) = 4, f(-1) = 1, f(0) = 0, and f(1) = 1. Therefore the Riemann sum is:

$$(1)(4+1+0+1) = 6.$$

b. The right-hand endpoints of the four subintervals are -1, 0, 1, and 2. We have f(-1) = 1, f(0) = 0, f(1) = 1, and f(2) = 4. So the Riemann sum is:

$$(1)(1+0+1+4) = 6.$$

c. The midpoints of the four subintervals are -1.5, -0.5, 0.5, and 1.5. We have f(-1.5) = 2.25, f(-0.5) = 0.25, f(0.5) = 0.25, and f(1.5) = 2.25. So the Riemann sum is:

$$(1)(2.25+0.25+0.25+2.25) = 5$$

(Note that the actual value of $\int_{-2}^{2} x^2 dx$, found by antidifferentiation, is $\frac{16}{3}$.)

The answers to the three parts of the example above would have been closer to the actual area, if we had split the interval $[-2,2]$ into a larger number of subintervals. For example, if we had chosen n = 150, we would have come up with 5.333096296 by choosing the midpoint of each subinterval. Of course, using n = 150 is not reasonable unless you have a computer or programmable calculator.

It is important to remember that not all functions have antiderivatives which can be written down in terms of the elementary functions we are familiar with, such as polynomials, roots, rational functions, exponential functions, logarithmic functions, and trigonometric functions. In such cases a Riemann sum approximation, or some similar method, is the only way to calculate the area. The next Part will discuss several methods for calculating such approximations.

Definite Integrals. Exercise 3. Riemann Sums.

For each problem, find the Riemann Sum with:

(a) x_k = left - hand endpoint

(b) x_k = right - hand endpoint

(c) x_k = midpoint.

1. x^3, $[0,3]$, n = 3.

2. x^3, $[0,3]$, n = 6.

3. $(x+1)^5$, $[-1,1]$, n = 4.

4. e^{x^2}, $[-1,2]$, n = 6.

5. sin x, $[0,4]$, n = 4.

6. sin x, $[0,\pi]$, n = 6.

7. ln x, $[1,10]$, n = 6.

8. $\frac{x+1}{x-1}$, $[2,4]$, n = 8.

9. $x^2 e^x \tan y$, $[(0,1)]$, n = 4.

10. $\sqrt{x^2 + x + 1}$, $[2,10]$, n = 8.

Approximation of Definite Integrals

In the previous part, we showed how a definite integral can be approximated by a Riemann sum. In this part, we will develop some additional methods for approximating the value of a definite integral. These methods are especially useful when the function is difficult or impossible to antidifferentiate.

Our first method, called the Midpoint Rule, was introduced in the last example of the previous Part. The idea is to divide the entire interval $[a, b]$ into some specified number of subintervals. For each subinterval, we will calculate the area of a rectangle whose width is the width of the subinterval, and whose height is the height of the graph at the midpoint of the subinterval. Then we add together the areas of all those rectangles.

Procedure for approximating $\int_a^b f(x)dx$ using the Midpoint Rule:

---

1. Let n = the number of subintervals you want to use. The larger n is, the more accurate your answer will be. On the other hand, a larger n makes the calculations longer.

2. Calculate $d = \frac{b-a}{n}$.

3. Calculate $x_1 = a + \frac{d}{2}$.

4. Calculate $x_2 = x_1 + d$,
   $x_3 = x_2 + d$, etc.
   Keep going until you get to x_n. If you calculated correctly, x_n will be equal to $(b - \frac{d}{2})$.

5. Substitute each x_k into f to find the values of $f(x_1)$, $f(x_2)$, etc.

6. Using the values you calculated above, the approximation you want is given by the formula:

$$d\left(\sum_{k=1}^{n} f(k_k)\right)$$

Example:

Approximate $\int_1^4 x^2 dx$, using the Midpoint Rule with n = 5.

SOLUTION:

The number of subintervals is already specified, so the first step is to calculate d. We have:

$$d = \frac{b-a}{n} = \frac{4-1}{5} = 0.6.$$

Now we calculate $x_1 = a + \frac{d}{2}$

$$= 1 + 0.3$$

$$= 1.3$$

Then, $x_2 = x_1 + d$
$$= 1.3 + 0.6$$
$$= 1.9$$

By using similar calculations, we get $x_3 = 2.5$, $x_4 = 3.1$, and $x_5 = 3.7$.

Substituting each x into the function $f(x) = x^2$, we get:

$$f(x_1) = 1.3^2 = 1.69$$
$$f(x_2) = 1.9^2 = 3.61$$
$$f(x_3) = 2.5^2 = 6.25$$
$$f(x_4) = 3.1^2 = 9.61$$
$$f(x_5) = 3.7^2 = 13.69$$

Adding up all the function values to get the value of $\sum_{k=1}^{5} f(x_k)$, we find the sum is 34.85.

Finally, we multiply the sum by d = 0.6, and arrive at our answer: 0.6(34.85) = 20.91.

Some people find it easier to keep track of the calculations if they use a chart like the one here:

x	x_k	$f(x_k)$
1	1.3	1.69
2	1.9	3.61
3	2.5	6.25
4	3.1	9.61
5	3.7	13.69
	Sum:	34.85

Another method of approximating a definite integral is called the Trapezoidal Rule. In this procedure, the idea is to divide the interval up into n subintervals as in the midpoint rule, but this time calculate the area for each subinterval as the area of a right trapezoid, with the height one side being the height of the graph at the left-hand endpoint of the subinterval, and the height at the other side being the height of the graph at the right-hand endpoint of the subinterval:

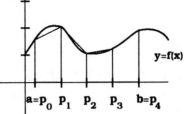

The formula for the area of a right trapezoid whose base has length d, and whose heights at the left and right sides are h_1 and h_2 respectively, is:

$$A = \frac{d(h_1+h_2)}{2}$$

Just as in the Midpoint Rule, the height of the graph at x = c is f(c). So this method requires us to use the values $f(p_k)$, where the p 's are the endpoints of the subintervals. We won't go explicitly through all the algebra required to derive the formula for the Trapezoidal Rule (it isn't hard, and the reader is encouraged to try it for her/himself). However, we make two observations from the diagram above: First, the total number of endpoints of the subintervals will be one more than the number of subintervals. In the diagram above, for example, there are four subintervals but five endpoints. Therefore, we will number the p_k's starting with p_0 instead of p_1. Secondly, the very first endpoint (which will be a) and the last endpoint (which is b) are used only in the first and last trapezoids respectively. Every other endpoint of a subinterval will be used first as the right-hand boundary of a trapezoid, and then as the left-hand boundary of the next trapezoid. This accounts for the difference in the way the first and last endpoints (p_0 and p_n) are handled.

Procedure for approximating $\int_a^b f(x)dx$ using the Trapezoidal Rule:

> 1. Let n = the number of subintervals you want to use, as in the Midpoint Rule.
>
> 2. Calculate $d = \frac{b-a}{2}$, just as in the Midpoint Rule.
>
> 3. Start with p_0 = a. Then calculate the other p 's by:
> $$p_1 = p_0 + d$$
> $$p_2 = p_1 + d, \text{ etc.}$$
>
>   Notice that, once you get the first p (which is p_0, or a), then the procedure is identical to the procedure for calculating the x 's in the Midpoint Rule. You just add d to the previous one each time.
>
> 4. Substitute each p into f(x) to find the values of $f(p_0)$, $f(p_1)$, $f(p_2)$, etc.
>
> 5. Using the values you calculated above, the approximation you want is given by the formula:
> $$\int_a^b f(x)dx \approx \frac{d}{2}\left[\left(f(p_0) + f(p_n)\right) + \sum_{k=1}^{n-1} 2f(p_k)\right].$$

53

Example:

Approximate $\int_5^8 \ln x \, dx$ by using the Trapezoidal Rule with n = 6.

SOLUTION:

First we calculate $d = \frac{8-5}{6} = 0.5$. Then we prepare a chart similar to the one shown in the Midpoint Rule example. This time, there is an extra column for the multiple of each function value (they all get multiplied by two except for the first one, $f(p_0)$, and the last one, $f(p_n)$):

k	p	f(p)	Multiple
0	5	1.6094	1.6094
1	5.5	1.7047	3.4094
2	6	1.7918	3.5836
3	6.5	1.8718	3.7436
4	7	1.9459	3.8918
5	7.5	2.0149	4.0298
6	8	2.0749	2.0794

$$\text{Total} \qquad 22.3470 = \left(f(p_0) + f(p_n) + \sum_{k=1}^{n-1} 2f(p_k) \right)$$

Now we multiply by $\frac{d}{2}$, or 0.25, to get the final answer:

$$22.3470 \times 0.25 = 5.5868$$

If we had done the problem by antidifferentiation to get an exact answer, the answer would have been 5.5883.

SIMPSON'S RULE:

Simpson's Rule is a third method of approximating a definite integral, and is usually more accurate than either of the two rules we have discussed so far. The idea of Simpson's Rule is this: Given any three points in the xy-plane, it is a fact that there is a quadratic or a linear function whose graph goes through all three points. So we once again divide our interval $[a, b]$ into subintervals. Then we find the x- and y-coordinates of the left endpoint, the right endpoint, and the midpoint of each subinterval. We find a quadratic or linear function whose graph goes through all three of those points, and use that function as an approximation to our original function (on that one subinterval only). Since quadratic and linear functions are easy to antidifferentiate, we can calculate the definite integral for the approximating function on the subinterval, and use the answer as an approximation to the definite integral of the original function. Adding up the approximations for each subinterval gives us an approximation for the definite integral of the original function on the entire interval.

Messy algebra is required to derive a formula for the approximate value of $\int_a^b f(x)dx$ using Simpson's rule. So we simply present the formula.

Let $x_1, x_2, \ldots, x_n$, be the values used for the Midpoint Rule, and $p_0, p_1, \ldots p_n$ be the values used for the Trapezoidal Rule. Then Simpson's Rule says that:

$$\int_a^b f(x)dx \approx \frac{d}{6}\left(f(p_0) + f(p_n) + \sum_{k=1}^{n} 4f(x_k) + \sum_{k=1}^{n-1} 2f(p_k) \right)$$

Even the formula above is a bit complicated, so there is still an easier one:

To calculate $\int_a^b f(x)dx$ with Simpson's rule, first find approximate answers with both the Midpoint Rule and with the Trapezoidal Rule, using the same "n" for both. Let M = the Midpoint approximation, and T = the Trapezoidal approximation. Then the Simpson's Rule approximation will be:

$$\frac{2M+T}{3}.$$

Simpson's Rule tends to be more accurate than either the Midpoint Rule or the Trapezoidal Rule, as we can see in the next example.

Example:

Estimate $\int_7^{10} e^{\sqrt{x}}dx$ by using the Midpoint Rule, the Trapezoidal Rule, and Simpson's Rule, all with n = 3.

SOLUTION:

By following the procedures given earlier, we find that d = 1, and that the table below will give us all the information we need:

x value	function value	Multiple (Trapezoidal)	Multiple (Simpson's)
x_1 = 7.5	15.4655		61.8621
x_2 = 8.5	18.4576		73.8304
x_3 = 9.5	21.8065		87.2259
p_0 = 7.0	14.0940	14.0940	14.0940
p_1 = 8.0	16.9188	33.8377	33.8377
p_2 = 9.0	20.0855	40.1711	40.1711
p_3 = 10.0	23.6243	23.6243	23.6243

The "multiple" values for the Trapezoidal Rule were obtained by multiplying $f(p_0)$ and $f(p_3)$ by 1, and $f(p_1)$ and $f(p_2)$ by 2. The values for Simpson's Rule were obtained by multiplying the function values for x_1, x_2, and x_3 by 4, and the values for p_1 and p_2 by 2.

For the Midpoint Rule, we add up the first three numbers in the "function value" column and multiply by $d = 1$, which gives us an answer of 55.7296.

For the Trapezoidal Rule, we add up the 4 numbers in the Trapezoidal Multiple column, which gives an answer of 111.7271. Then we multiply by $\frac{d}{2} = 0.5$, which gives a final answer of 55.8636.

For Simpson's Rule, we could go the long way and add up the Simpson Multiple column, which gives 334.6455; and then multiply by $\frac{d}{6} = \frac{1}{6}$, which gives a final answer of 55.7743.

We could also use the second version of Simpson's Rule, which would have given the calculation:

$$\frac{2M+T}{3} = \frac{167.3228}{3} = 55.7743.$$

We might expect that using only three subintervals will give us a very rough answer. But the fact is that if we had used $n = 150$, the (Simpson's Rule) answer would be 55.77424082. If we had done no rounding off, with $n = 3$, Simpson's would have given us 55.77424248 - an error of only .000061 %!

Definite Integrals. Exercise 4. Approximation of Definite Integrals.

In problems 1-6, approximate the value of the definite integral with the Midpoint Rule, the Trapezoidal Rule, and Simpson's Rule. The number of subintervals to be used is given. Then, compare your answer to the actual value obtained by antidifferentiation. Use at least six significant digits for all calculations.

1. $\int_{-1}^{1} e^x dx$, $n = 4$

2. $\int_{1}^{4} x^2 dx$, $n = 6$

3. $\int_{3}^{4} \sin x\, dx$, $n = 5$

4. $\int_{-2}^{2} \frac{2x+1}{\sqrt[3]{x^2+x+4}}\, dx$, $n = 5$

5. $\int_{1}^{8} \ln x\, dx$, $n = 7$

6. $\int_{0}^{4}\left(x^2 - e^x\right) dx$, $n = 8$

In problems 7-13, use all three methods of approximation to estimate the value of the integral.

7. $\int_0^2 \sin^2\left(4 - 5x^3\right)dx, \quad n = 4$

11. $\int_5^7 x^{\frac{3}{2}} \tan\left(\frac{x}{50}\right)dx, \quad n = 4$

8. $\int_0^3 \sqrt{\frac{x^2+1}{x+1}}\, dx, \quad n = 6$

12. $\int_{.6\pi}^{1.2\pi} \tan x \, dx, \quad n = 6$

9. $\int_0^3 e^{x^2}\, dx, \quad n = 6$

13. $\int_2^3 \frac{\ln x}{\cos(2x+1)}dx, \quad n = 5$

10. $\int_2^5 \frac{e^x - 10}{\ln x}dx, \quad n = 6$

14. $\int_2^5 \frac{\ln x}{\cos(2x+1)}dx, \quad n = 6$

Why are the three answers so different? Are they a reasonable approximation of the actual value?

| Part 5 | **Areas Between Two or More Curves** |

The procedure for calculating the area between a curve and the x-axis can easily be generalized so that we can find the area between two different graphs. The simplest case is where we want the area between the graphs of y = f(x) and y = g(x), bounded by the vertical lines x = a and x = b, where f(x) is greater than or equal to g(x) on the entire interval [a,b].

Example:

Find the area between the graph of $y = e^{\frac{1}{4}x}$ and $y = \ln x$, from x = 2 to x = 6.

SOLUTION:

We are asked for Area A in this diagram.

Notice that $\int_2^6 e^{\frac{x}{4}}dx$ is Area A + Area B,

and $\int_2^6 \ln x \, dx$ is Area B. Therefore:

$A = A + B - B$

$= \int_2^6 e^{\frac{x}{4}}dx - \int_2^6 \ln x \, dx$

$= \left(4e^{\frac{x}{4}} - (x\ln x - x)\right)\Big|_2^6$

$= (17.9268 - 4.7506) - (6.5949 - (-0.6137))$

$= 13.1762 - 7.2086$

$= 5.9676$

If the graphs of two continuous functions intersect in exactly two points, then it is not necessary to be given the x values of the left and right boundaries of the region.

Example:

Find the area of the region enclosed by the graphs of the following functions:

$$f(x) = -2x + 27$$
$$g(x) = -x^2 + 10x + 7$$

SOLUTION:

We can find the point(s) where the two graphs intersect by setting the two functions equal to each other and solving:

$$-2x + 27 = -x^2 + 10x + 7$$

The solutions are x = 2 and x = 10. Therefore, the limits of integration which we use to solve this problem will be 2 and 10.

As in the previous example, we will integrate the "upper" function minus the "lower" function, this time from x = 2 to x = 10. Last time, we used a graph to decide which was the upper function. This time, unless we want to graph the two functions ourselves, we will need another method. The simplest thing to do is to just substitute some number between 2 and 10 into both functions. The function which gives us a larger answer must be the upper function. So we choose x = 5, and find that

$$f(5) = 17$$
$$g(5) = 32$$

Therefore, $g(x) = -x^2 + 10x + 7$ is the upper function, and $f(x) = -2x + 27$ is the lower. Our integral is therefore:

$$\int_2^{10} \left((-x^2 + 10x + 7) - (-2x + 27) \right) dx$$

$$= \int_2^{10} \left(-x^2 + 12x - 20 \right) dx$$

$$= -\frac{1}{3}x^3 + 6x^2 - 20x \Big|_2^{10}$$

$$= \frac{200}{3} - \left(-\frac{56}{3} \right) = \frac{256}{3}$$

A graph of this problem is shown here.

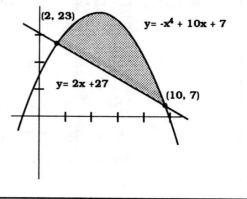

58

It is easy to verify that the rule of "upper function minus lower function" is valid even when one or both graphs go below the x-axis.

Example:

Find the area of the region bounded by the graphs of:

$$f(x) = -x^2 + 4x + 10$$
$$g(x) = x^2 - 2x - 10$$

SOLUTION:

If we set $f(x) = g(x)$ and solve, the solutions are $x = -2$ and $x = 5$. Since 0 is between -2 and 5, we can substitute 0 into f and g and see immediately that $f(0) = 10$, and $g(0) = -10$. Therefore f is the upper function and g is the lower. Our calculations are now:

$$\int_{-2}^{5}\left((-x^2 + 4x + 10) - (x^2 - 2x - 10)\right)dx$$

$$= \int_{-2}^{5}\left(-2x^2 + 6x + 20\right)dx$$

$$= -\frac{2}{3}x^3 + 3x^2 - 20x\Big|_{-2}^{5}$$

$$= \frac{275}{3} - \left(-\frac{68}{3}\right) = \frac{343}{3}$$

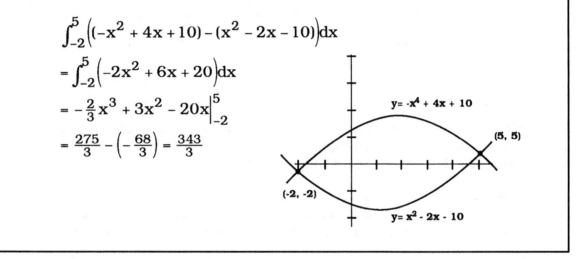

Sometimes one graph will cross over another more than twice, creating more than one bounded region. In that case, the upper function for one region may turn out to be the lower function for another region. To solve such problems, we need to calculate the area of each region separately, and then add the areas together.

Example:

Find the area of the closed region(s) bounded by the graphs of:

$$y = f(x) = -x^3 + 4x^2 + 7x - 6$$
$$\text{and } y = 4.$$

SOLUTION:

If we set $-x^3 + 4x^2 + 7x - 6$ equal to 4, we get 3 solutions: -2, 1, and 5. Since $f(0) = -6$, which is less than 4, the upper function from -2 to 1 is the constant number 4. On the other hand, $f(3) = 24$, which is greater than 4, so that on the interval (1,5), the upper function will be $f(x)$.

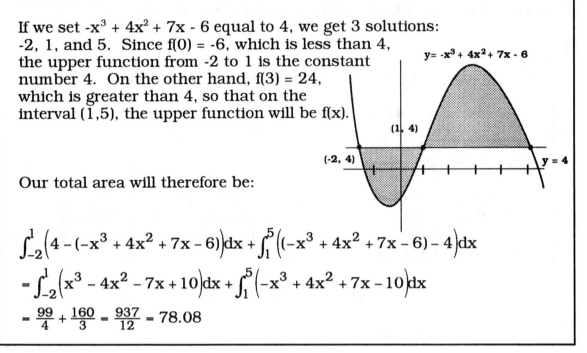

Our total area will therefore be:

$$\int_{-2}^{1}\left(4 - (-x^3 + 4x^2 + 7x - 6)\right)dx + \int_{1}^{5}\left((-x^3 + 4x^2 + 7x - 6) - 4\right)dx$$

$$= \int_{-2}^{1}\left(x^3 - 4x^2 - 7x + 10\right)dx + \int_{1}^{5}\left(-x^3 + 4x^2 + 7x - 10\right)dx$$

$$= \frac{99}{4} + \frac{160}{3} = \frac{937}{12} = 78.08$$

We can continue to complicate our lives, this time by considering regions bounded by three or more graphs. These can become complicated, and almost always require the help of the graph itself to look at.

Example:

Find the area of the closed region bounded by the graphs of:

$$y = x + 2$$
$$y = 5 - 2x$$
$$y = x^2 - 4x + 2.$$

SOLUTION:

The situation is shown in the graph below. As we can see, the region we are talking about is actually the sum of two regions. In the first region, the upper function is $x + 2$, and the lower function is $x^2 - 4x + 2$. In the second region, the upper function is $5 - 2x$, and the lower one is still $x^2 - 4x + 2$.

Before we can calculate the areas by antidifferentiation, we need to figure out where the points of intersection A, B, and C are. Point A is the intersection of $y = x + 2$ and $y = x^2 - 4x + 2$. Setting those two functions equal to each other, we get two solutions: 0 and 5. It is clear from the diagram that A is the point where $x = 0$ (the other point of intersection, where $x = 5$, is off to the right of the graph).

60

The point B is the intersection between $y = x + 2$ and $y = 5 - 2x$. Setting those two expressions equal to each other gives the solution $x = 1$.

Point C is the intersection between $y = 5 - 2x$ and $y = x^2 - 4x + 2$. The solutions to $5 - 2x = x^2 - 4x + 2$ are -1 and 3. We can see from the graph that the point C is where $x = 3$.

Our calculations show that the first region goes from $x = 0$ on the left to $x = 1$ on the right, with $x + 2$ as the upper function and $x^2 - 4x + 2$ as the lower function. The second region goes from $x = 1$ on the left to $x = 3$ on the right, with $5 - 2x$ as the upper function and $x^2 - 4x + 2$ as the lower. Accordingly, the total area is:

$$\int_0^1 \left((x + 2) - (x^2 - 4x + 2) \right) dx + \int_1^3 \left((5 - 2x) - (x^2 - 4x + 2) \right) dx$$

$$= \frac{13}{6} + \frac{16}{3}$$

$$= 7.5$$

Definite Integrals. Exercise 5. Areas Between Curves.

1. Find the area between the graphs of $x + 2$ and $\sin x$, from $x = 0$ to $x = 2\pi$.

2. Find the area of the region enclosed by the graph of $-\frac{8}{x}$ and $x - 6$.

3. Find the area of the region enclosed by the graphs of x (that is, $y = x$), $-4 - x$, and $0.5x + 3$.

4. Find the area between the graphs of $x^2 + 6x + 20$ and $-x^2 - 8x - 17$, from $x = -5$ to $x = -2$.

5. Find the area of the region enclosed by the graph of $3x + 10$ and x^2.

6. Find the area of the region enclosed by the x-axis and $y = \sin x$, from $x = 0$ to $x = 2\pi$.

7. Find the area of the region enclosed by the graphs of $5 - x^2$, $x - 1$, and $-x - 1$.

8. Find the area between the graphs of 2^x and $-x$, from $x = 1$ to $x = 4$.

9. Find the area of the region enclosed by the graphs $x^2 - 4$ and $-x^2 + 4$.

10. Find the area of the region enclosed by the graphs of $y = 4$, and $y = x^2 + 2$.

11. Find the area between the graphs of $\frac{10}{x}$ and $x^2 + 8$, from $x = 2$ to $x = 6$.

12. Find the area of the region enclosed by the graphs of $x - 8$ and $\ln x$.

13. Find the area of the region enclosed by the graphs of $y = x$ and $y = x^3 - 3x$.

14. Find the area of the quadrilateral whose four sides are the graphs of x, -x, 5x-30, and 12 - 2x.

Average Value of a Function

The area of a rectangle is given by the formula

$$A = wh$$

where w = the width of the rectangle, and h = the height. If we rearrange the formula slightly to solve for h, we get

$$h = \frac{A}{w}$$

In other words, we can find the height of a rectangle if we know both the area and the width.

Suppose we have a region which is rectangular on three sides, but with an irregular upper boundary. The irregularity of the top means that the height of the region will vary from one point to another. But if we know both the area and the width of the region, we can use the formula above to calculate the **average** height of the region.

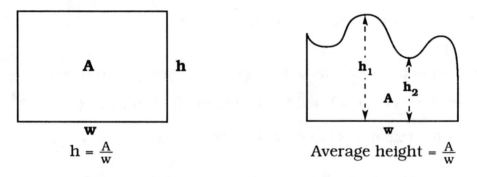

$$h = \frac{A}{w}$$
Average height $= \frac{A}{w}$.

Now suppose the region we are interested in is the area bounded by the x-axis, the vertical lines x = a and x = b, and the graph of y = f(x). Then the width of the region is b - a, and the area is $\int_a^b f(x)\,dx$. Therefore the average height of the region is given by the formula:

$$\text{Average height} \;=\; \frac{A}{W} \;=\; \frac{1}{b\text{-}a} \int_a^b f(x)\,dx.$$

But the height of the region at any point x = c is simply f(c). So the formula above is actually giving us the average value of f(x) on the interval [a,b].

Let f(x) be a function which is continuous on the interval [a,b].
Then the <u>average value</u> of f(x) on the interval [a,b] is:

$$\frac{1}{b\text{-}a} \int_a^b f(x)\,dx.$$

Example:

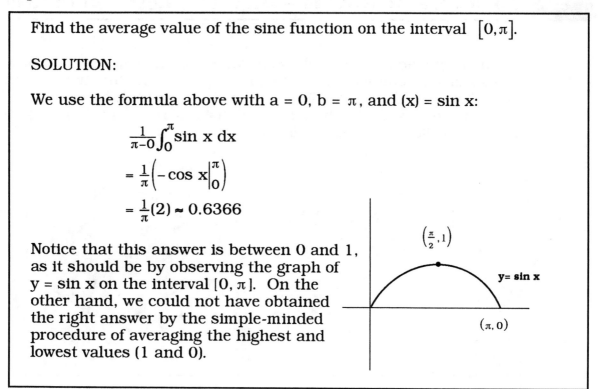

Find the average value of the sine function on the interval $[0,\pi]$.

SOLUTION:

We use the formula above with $a = 0$, $b = \pi$, and $(x) = \sin x$:

$$\frac{1}{\pi - 0}\int_0^\pi \sin x \, dx$$

$$= \frac{1}{\pi}\left(-\cos x \Big|_0^\pi\right)$$

$$= \frac{1}{\pi}(2) \approx 0.6366$$

Notice that this answer is between 0 and 1, as it should be by observing the graph of $y = \sin x$ on the interval $[0, \pi]$. On the other hand, we could not have obtained the right answer by the simple-minded procedure of averaging the highest and lowest values (1 and 0).

Definite Integrals. Exercise 6. The Average Value of a Function.

In each case, find the average value of the given function on the given interval.

1. $x\cos x$, $\left[-1, \frac{\pi}{2}\right]$

2. e^{4-3x}, $[-2,2]$

3. $x^2 \ln(1-x)^2$, $[-5,-3]$

4. $\frac{-1}{1+x^2}$, $[0,2]$

5. $3x^3 - 8x$, $[5,6]$

6. $\frac{1}{x^2-4}$, $[-1.9,1.9]$ Why can't we use the interval $[-1.9,2.1]$?

7. $\sqrt{2x+1}$, $[0,4]$

8. $\frac{\ln x}{x}$, $[15,20]$

9. $\ln(12x - 1)$, $[15,20]$

10. xe^{5x}, $[-2,1]$

63

Let us take a region of the x-y plane, bounded on the left and right by x = a and x = b respectively, bounded above by the graph of some function f(x), and bounded below by the x-axis. We then revolve the region around the x-axis (in three-dimensional space). The three-dimensional region generated by that revolution is called a *solid of revolution*.

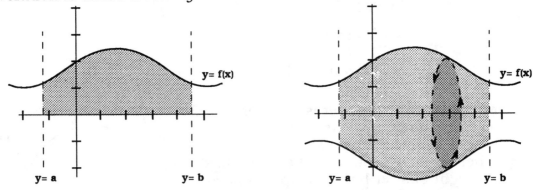

Example:

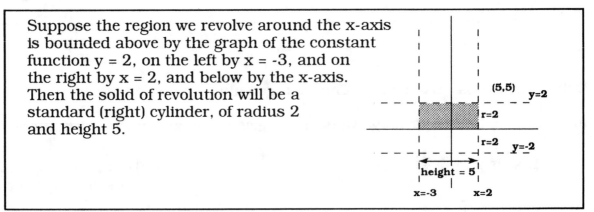

Suppose the region we revolve around the x-axis is bounded above by the graph of the constant function y = 2, on the left by x = -3, and on the right by x = 2, and below by the x-axis. Then the solid of revolution will be a standard (right) cylinder, of radius 2 and height 5.

We can calculate the volume of a solid of revolution by slicing the solid into very thin slices with a knife whose blade is perpendicular to both the x-axis and to the x-y plane itself. If we examine the slice which is centered at x = c, we will see that the face of the disk is a circle of radius approximately f(c) (see the diagrams above), and therefore the face of the slice has an approximate area of $\pi r^2 = \pi f(c))^2$.

The volume of the slice is the area of the face, multiplied by the thickness. If we allow the number of slices to increase without limit (so that the thickness of each slice approaches zero), the sum of the volumes of all the slices will be:

$$\int_a^b \pi(f(x))^2 \, dx$$

or

$$\pi \int_a^b (f(x))^2 \, dx$$

Example:

Find the volume of the solid obtained by revolving the area bounded by the x-axis, the graph of $y = 1 - \frac{1}{2}x$, and the y-axis around the x-axis.

SOLUTION:

First, we note that the solid obtained by revolving the given area around the x-axis is a cone, tipped over horizontally. The "height" (from left to right) of the cone is 2, and the radius of the base (the circular slice parallel to the y-axis) is 1.

radius of cone = 1

height of cone = 2 $y=1-\frac{1}{2}x$

The formula for the volume of a cone of height h and whose base has radius r is:

$$V = \frac{\pi r^2 h}{3}$$

Therefore we expect our answer to be $\frac{\pi(1^2)(2)}{3} = \frac{2\pi}{3}$.

If we do the problem with the integral formula given earlier, we have:

$$a = 0$$
$$b = 2$$
$$f(x) = 1 - \frac{1}{2}x$$

and therefore the volume is equal to $\pi \int_0^2 \left(1 - \frac{1}{2}x\right)^2 dx$. This integral can be evaluated either with the substitution $u = 1 - \frac{1}{2}x$, or by multiplying out $\left(1 - \frac{1}{2}x\right)^2$, and integrating term by term. In either case, the answer is $\frac{2\pi}{3}$ ust as predicted.

We should note that most solids of revolution are not nice regular geometric shapes like cylinders or cones. So we usually have no alternative to calculating the volume with integrals.

We can now complicate the situation by asking what happens if we revolve a graph around a horizontal line other than the x-axis (the line around which we revolve the region will be called the axis of revolution). The equation of any horizontal line is y = k, where k is some constant (in the case of the x-axis, k is zero). If we revolve the graph of y = f(x) around the line y = k, from x = a to x = b, the volume of the resulting solid of revolution is:

$$V = \pi \int_a^b (f(x) - k)^2 dx$$

Example:

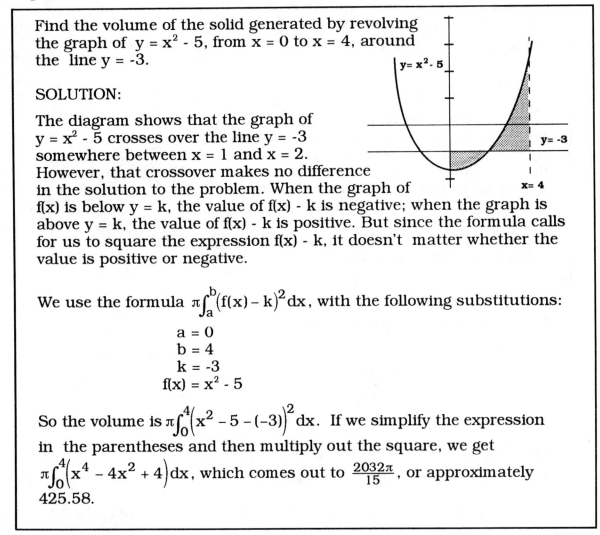

Find the volume of the solid generated by revolving the graph of $y = x^2 - 5$, from $x = 0$ to $x = 4$, around the line $y = -3$.

y= x²- 5

y= -3

x= 4

SOLUTION:

The diagram shows that the graph of $y = x^2 - 5$ crosses over the line $y = -3$ somewhere between $x = 1$ and $x = 2$. However, that crossover makes no difference in the solution to the problem. When the graph of $f(x)$ is below $y = k$, the value of $f(x) - k$ is negative; when the graph is above $y = k$, the value of $f(x) - k$ is positive. But since the formula calls for us to square the expression $f(x) - k$, it doesn't matter whether the value is positive or negative.

We use the formula $\pi\int_a^b (f(x) - k)^2 dx$, with the following substitutions:

$$a = 0$$
$$b = 4$$
$$k = -3$$
$$f(x) = x^2 - 5$$

So the volume is $\pi\int_0^4 \left(x^2 - 5 - (-3)\right)^2 dx$. If we simplify the expression in the parentheses and then multiply out the square, we get $\pi\int_0^4 \left(x^4 - 4x^2 + 4\right) dx$, which comes out to $\frac{2032\pi}{15}$, or approximately 425.58.

Now we introduce a further complication: we want to revolve the region <u>between</u> two graphs around some horizontal line in the x-y plane, and calculate the volume of the resulting solid. The solid will have a "hole" in the center since the region being revolved does not reach all the way to the axis of revolution. The formula we give below requires some restrictions on the behavior of $f(x)$ and $g(x)$, but it isn't too hard to adapt the formula for other situations.

Suppose either $k \le g(x) \le f(x)$ or $f(x) \le g(x) \le k$ for all x between a and b. If we revolve the region of the plane bounded by $x = a$, $x = b$, $y = f(x)$, and $y = g(x)$, around the horizontal line $y = k$, the volume of the resulting solid is given by the formula:

$$V = \pi\int_a^b \left[(f(x) - k)^2 - (g(x) - k)^2 dx\right].$$

Example:

Find the volume of the solid of revolution which results from revolving the region enclosed between $y = -x^2 + 6x + 1$ and $y = 7 - x$ around the line $y = -3$.

SOLUTION:

The region enclosed between the two functions $-x^2 + 6x + 1$ and $7 - x$ is bounded by the x-values of the two points of intersection. If we set

$$-x^2 + 6x + 1 = 7 - x$$

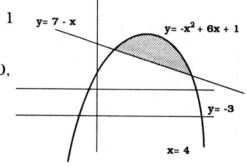

and solve, we find the solutions are $x = 1$ and $x = 6$. If we substitute $x = 3$ (a number between 1 and 6) into both functions, we find that $-x^2 + 6x + 1 = 10$, and $7 - x = 4$. We are revolving the region around the line $y = -3$, so $k = -3$. Putting that information together, we have:

$$-3 \leq 7 - x \leq -x^2 + 6x + 1$$

So we will use our formula with:

$$a = 1$$
$$b = 6$$
$$k = -3$$
$$f(x) = -x^2 + 6x - 1$$
$$g(x) = 7 - x$$

The calculations are:

$$\pi \int_1^6 \left[\left(-x^2 + 6x + 1 - (-3) \right)^2 - (7 - x - (-3))^2 \right] dx$$

$$= \pi \int_1^6 \left[(x^4 - 12x^3 + 28x^2 + 48x + 16) - (100 - 20x + x^2) \right] dx$$

$$= \pi \int_1^6 (x^4 - 12x^3 + 27x^2 + 68x - 84) dx$$

$$= 375\pi$$

$$\approx 1178.10$$

The volumes of some solids of revolution can be calculated only by dividing the region to be revolved into two or more sub-regions.

Example:

Find the volume of the solid of revolution generated by revolving the region bounded by the y-axis and the graphs of $y = 4$, $y = 1$, and $y = x^2$, around the x-axis.

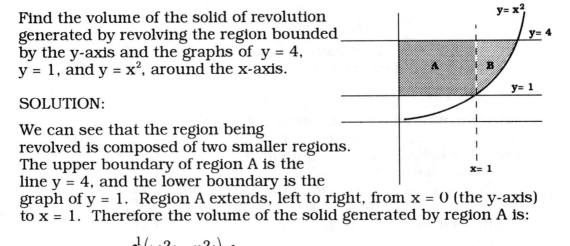

SOLUTION:

We can see that the region being revolved is composed of two smaller regions. The upper boundary of region A is the line $y = 4$, and the lower boundary is the graph of $y = 1$. Region A extends, left to right, from $x = 0$ (the y-axis) to $x = 1$. Therefore the volume of the solid generated by region A is:

$$\pi \int_0^1 \left((4^2) - (1^2) \right) dx$$

$$= \pi \left(15x \Big|_0^1 \right)$$

$$= 15\pi.$$

The upper boundary of region B is still the line $y = 4$, but the lower boundary is the graph of $y = x^2$. From left to right, region B extends from $x = 1$ to $x = 2$. Therefore the volume of the solid of revolution generated by region B is:

$$\pi \int_1^2 \left((4^2) - (x^2)^2 \right) dx$$

$$= \pi \left(16x - \frac{x^5}{5} \right) \Big|_1^2$$

$$= \frac{49\pi}{5}$$

Therefore the volume of the entire solid of revolution is the sum of the volumes of the two solids generated by regions A and B, or

$$15\pi + \frac{49\pi}{5}$$

$$= \frac{124}{5}\pi$$

$$\approx 77.9.$$

If a region of the x-y plane is being revolved around a vertical line, we can often adapt the earlier formulas to calculate the volume of the resulting solid.

Example:

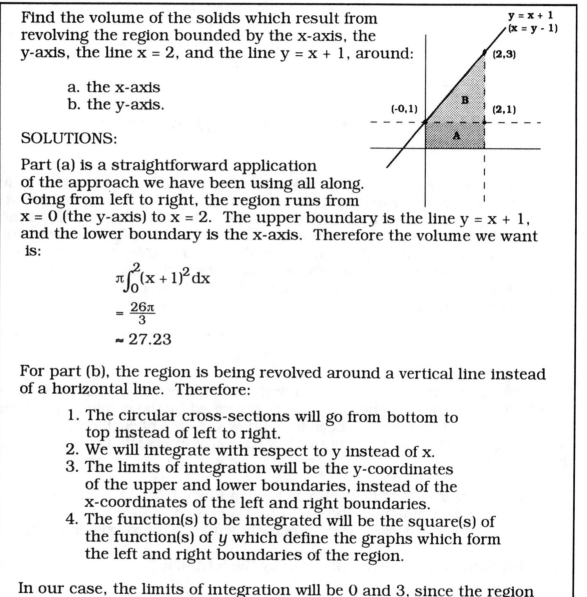

Find the volume of the solids which result from revolving the region bounded by the x-axis, the y-axis, the line x = 2, and the line y = x + 1, around:

       a. the x-axis
       b. the y-axis.

SOLUTIONS:

Part (a) is a straightforward application of the approach we have been using all along. Going from left to right, the region runs from x = 0 (the y-axis) to x = 2. The upper boundary is the line y = x + 1, and the lower boundary is the x-axis. Therefore the volume we want is:

$$\pi \int_0^2 (x+1)^2 dx$$

$$= \frac{26\pi}{3}$$

$$\approx 27.23$$

For part (b), the region is being revolved around a vertical line instead of a horizontal line. Therefore:

1. The circular cross-sections will go from bottom to top instead of left to right.
2. We will integrate with respect to y instead of x.
3. The limits of integration will be the y-coordinates of the upper and lower boundaries, instead of the x-coordinates of the left and right boundaries.
4. The function(s) to be integrated will be the square(s) of the function(s) of *y* which define the graphs which form the left and right boundaries of the region.

In our case, the limits of integration will be 0 and 3, since the region goes from 0 to 3 from bottom to top. The left and right boundaries, however, are a bit more trouble. From y = 0 (the x-axis) to y = 1, the left-hand boundary is the y-axis, or x = 0. However, from y = 1 to y = 3, the left-hand boundary is the line y = x + 1, or x = y - 1 (See note below). Therefore we have to divide the region up into two sub-regions A and B, as shown.

Region A: The y values run from 0 to 1. The right boundary is the constant 2, and the left boundary is the constant 0. Therefore the required integral is

$$\pi \int_0^1 (2)^2 dy = 4\pi$$

69

Region B: The y values run from 1 to 3. The right boundary is the constant 2, and the left boundary is the line x = y - 1. So the integral is:

$$\pi\int_1^3\left((2)^2 - (y-1)^2\right)dy$$

$$= \pi\left(\frac{-y^3}{3} + y^2 + 3y\bigg|_1^3\right)$$

$$= \frac{16\pi}{3}$$

Adding together the answers for the two regions, we get our final answer, $\frac{28\pi}{3} \approx 29.32$.

(NOTE on the selecting of boundaries: Geometrically, it would make just as much sense for us to say that the line x = y - 1 is the upper boundary for region B rather than the left boundary. In that case the left boundary would be x = 0 and the right boundary would be x = 2. However, when we are integrating with respect to y, the upper and lower boundaries have to be constant numbers, because those are going to be the limits of integration. Similarly, when we integrate with respect to x, we have to choose constant numbers as the left and right boundaries.)

Finally, we can extend our method to find the volumes of other objects. It is not always necessary for the object to be generated by the revolution of a region around a straight line. All we need is to know the area of each cross-section, or "slice." Suppose we can place our object so that it intersects the x-y plane in the following way:

1. The entire object lies between x = a and x = b.
2. There is a function, A(x), such that A(c) is the area of the vertical cross section perpendicular to the x-axis, at x = c.

Then, the volume of the object is given by the formula:

$$V = \int_a^b A(x)\,dx.$$

(Note that this formula is the same one we used for solids of revolution, when $A(x) = \pi(f(x))^2$).

Example:

Find a formula for the volume of a pyramid with a square base and height h, where the length of each side of the base is b.

SOLUTION:

If the pyramid is tipped over horizontally and placed conveniently in the the x-y planes, faces will look like the diagram below.

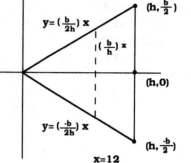

We can find the equations $y = \left(\frac{b}{2h}\right)x$ and $y = \left(\frac{-b}{2h}\right)x$ by calculating the slopes and then using the point-slope formula, using the fact that $(0, 0)$ is on both lines.. Each slice of the pyramid is a square. We can see from the diagram that the length of each side of the square x units from the origin (which is the tip of the pyramid) is $\left(\frac{b}{2h}\right)x - \left(\frac{-b}{2h}\right)x$, or $\left(\frac{b}{h}\right)x$.

Therefore the area of the square cross section is $A(x) = \left(\frac{b}{h}\right)^2 x^2$.

Using the formula above, we calculate:

$$V = \int_0^h \frac{b^2}{h^2}x^2 dx = \frac{b^2}{h^2}\left(\frac{x^3}{3}\bigg|_0^h\right)$$

$$= \frac{b^2 h^3}{3h^2}$$

$$= \frac{b^2 h}{3}.$$

Definite Integrals. Exercise 7. Volume of Solids—Disk and Washer Methods.

In problems 1-21, find the volume of the solid generated by revolving the region with the given boundaries around the given axis:

1. Boundaries: x-axis, $x = 1$, $x = 9$, $y = \frac{1}{\sqrt{x}}$. Axis: x-axis.
2. Boundaries: y-axis, $y = 5 - x$, $y = 2$, $y = 5$. Axis: y-axis.
3. Boundaries: x-axis, $x = \frac{3\pi}{4}$, $x = \frac{5\pi}{4}$, $y = \sec x$. Axis: x-axis.
4. Boundaries: $x = -2$, $x = 2$, $y = x^2$, $y = x^2 + 4$. Axis: x-axis.
5. Boundaries: x-axis, $x = 0$, $x = \pi$, $y = \sqrt{\sin x}$. Axis: x-axis.
6. Boundaries: x-axis, $y = \sqrt{4 - x^2}$, y = axis, $x = 2$. Axis: x-axis.
7. Boundaries: same as #6, plus the x-axis. Axis: y-axis.
8. Boundaries: y-axis, $y = 9$, $y = x^2$ for $x \geq 0$. Axis: y-axis.
9. Boundaries: same as #8. Axis: x-axis.
10. Boundaries: same as #8 and 9. Axis: $x = 4$.
11. Boundaries: same as #8-10. Axis: $y = -2$.
12. Boundaries: y-axis, x-axis, $\sqrt{x + 4}$, $x = 5$. Axis: x-axis.
13. Boundaries: same as #12. Axis: y-axis.
14. Boundaries: same as #12 and 13. Axis: $x = 5$.
15. Boundaries: same as #12-14. Axis: $y = 5$.
16. Boundaries: $y = e^x$, $x = 0$, $x = 2$, x-axis. Axis: x-axis.

71

17. Boundaries: same as #16. Axis: y-axis.
18. Boundaries: same as #16 and 17. Axis: x = -2
19. Boundaries: same as #16-19. Axis: y = 8.
20. Boundaries: $y = x^2$, $y = x + 2$. Axis: x-axis.
21. Boundaries: same as #20. Axis: x = 3.
22. Find the volume of a solid whose base is the region enclosed by $y = 1 - x^2$ and $y = x^2 - 1$, where the cross-sections perpendicular to the x-axis are: (a) squares, (b) rectangles of height 2, (c) equilateral triangles.

Part 8 — Volumes of Solids—Shell Method

There are some solids of revolution whose boundaries or axes make it difficult or impossible to calculate the volume with the disk or washer methods. In most such cases, the shell method, to be introduced in this Part, will enable us to find the desired volume.

The disk and washer methods were based on the idea of slicing the solid into a large number of circular slices (with holes in the middles for the washer method), and adding together the volumes of the thin circular slices. In effect, we took circular slices perpendicular to the axis of revolution, and moved parallel to the axis of revolution as we went from one slice to the next. The shell method uses a similar idea, except this time each thin piece will be a cylindrical shape with the axis of revolution as its center axis. As we move from one cylindrical shell to the next, we will be moving from the outside of the solid, in toward the axis of revolution. The volume of each thin cylindrical shell is then given by the formula:

$$V = 2\pi rh\Delta r$$

where r = radius of the cylinder
h = height of the cylinder
Δr = thickness of the shell

As we allow Δr to approach zero (and therefore the number of cylindrical shells approaches infinity), we get the formulas given below.

Suppose:
(1) The axis of revolution is vertical, and therefore has the equation x = c for some number c.
(2) The region to be revolved is bounded above by y = f(x), below by y = g(x), on the left by x = a, and on the right by x = b.
(3) The region being revolved lies entirely to the right of the axis of revolution. (If the region lies entirely to the left of the axis, then we can make the formula work by switching the f(x) with the g(x)).

Then the volume of the resulting solid of revolution is:

$$2\pi \int_a^b (x - c)(f(x) - g(x))dx$$

Similarly, suppose:

        (1) The axis of revolution is horizontal, and therefore has the equation $y = c$ for some number c.

        (2) The region to be revolved is bounded on the right by $x = f(y)$, on the left by $x = g(y)$, below by $y = a$, and above by $y = b$.

        (3) The region to be revolved lies entirely above the axis of revolution (if the region lies entirely below the axis, we can make the formula work by switching the f(y) with the g(y).

Then the volume of the resulting solid of revolution is:

$$2\pi\int_a^b (y - c)(f(y) - g(y))dy$$

EXAMPLE:

Find the volume of the solid of revolution formed by revolving around the y-axis the region bounded by $y = 3 - x^2$, the y-axis, and the positive x-axis.

(0, 3)
($\sqrt{3}$, 0)
$y = 3 - x^2$

SOLUTION:

We will solve this problem twice: First with the disk method and then with the shell method.

Disk method:

To use the disk method when the axis of revolution is the y-axis, we integrate with respect to y. This means that the right and left boundaries must be expressed as functions of x. The left boundary is the y-axis, whose equation is $x = 0$. The right boundary is the graph of $y = 3 - x^2$. If we solve that equation for x, we get $x = \sqrt{3 - y}$. (Note that if the region in question had been to the left of the y-axis, we would be using the function $x = -\sqrt{3 - y}$.) As we can see from the diagram, the upper boundary of the region is $y = 3$, and the lower boundary is $y = 0$ (the x-axis). Therefore the volume is calculated as:

$$V = \pi\int_0^3 \left(\sqrt{3 - y}\right)^2 dy$$

$$= \frac{9\pi}{2}.$$

Shell Method:

When using the shell method for a region being revolved around a vertical axis, we integrate with respect to x. Therefore the upper and lower boundaries must be functions of x. In this case, the upper boundary is already given as $y = 3 - x^2$, and the lower boundary (the x-axis) is $y = 0$. The left boundary (the y-axis) is $x = 0$, and the right boundary is $x = \sqrt{3}$ (see diagram). Using the letters given in the formula above, that means that $a = 0$, $b = \sqrt{3}$, and $c = 0$. Therefore the volume is:

$$2\pi\int_0^{\sqrt{3}} (x - 0)(3 - x^2)dx$$

$$= 2\pi\int_0^{\sqrt{3}} (3x - x^3)dx$$

$$= \frac{9\pi}{2}, \text{ just as before.}$$

As the preceding example shows, sometimes a volume problem can be done equally easily with discs (or washers) or with shells. However, there are several cases in which one method is definitely preferable to the other. For example, sometimes one method requires breaking the region up into two sub-regions to be calculated separately, whereas the other method can handle the entire region with one integral.

EXAMPLE:

Find the volume of the region generated by revolving around the line $y = -1$, the region bounded by the x-axis, the y-axis, and the lines $y = 2$ and $y = \frac{2}{3}x - \frac{4}{3}$.

SOLUTION:

If we want to use the disk/washer method for this problem, we will have to integrate with respect to x. This procedure requires that the upper and lower boundaries of the region be expressed as functions of x, and the left and right boundaries must be numerical values of x. By looking at the diagram, we can see that the lower boundary is just the x-axis for interval $0 \le x \le 2$, and the line $y = \frac{2}{3}x - \frac{4}{3}$ for the interval $2 \le x \le 5$ (we cannot use the line $y = \frac{2}{3}x - \frac{4}{3}$ as the right-hand boundary, because the right boundary has to be just a number). Although the two integrals involved are relatively easy to calculate, sheer human laziness makes us prefer a method which has only one integral.

The shell method allows us to calculate the volume with only one integral. When we have a horizontal axis of revolution, the shell method requires that we integrate with respect to y, which in turn means that upper and lower boundaries must be numbers, and the left and right boundaries are to be functions of y. If we solve the equation $y = \frac{2}{3}x - \frac{4}{3}$ for x, we get $x = \frac{3}{2}y + 2$. Therefore, our values for the shell method formula are:

a = 0 (lower boundary)
b = 2 (upper boundary)
c = -1

$f(y) = \frac{3}{2}y + 2$ (right boundary)

$g(y) = 0$ (left boundary = y-axis)

Making the appropriate substitutions into the formula, we find the volume is:

$$2\pi\int_0^2 (y - (-1))(\tfrac{3}{2}y + 2)dy$$
$$= 30\pi$$

The reader is invited to do the problem with the disk/washer method, splitting the region into two as discussed earlier, to see that the answer would be the same.

Another way to decide whether to use the shell or the disk method is to determine whether the boundaries can be easily expressed as functions of the proper variable.

EXAMPLE:

Find the volume of the solid generated by revolving around the y-axis the region bounded by the x-axis, the line x = 2, and the graph of $y = x + e^x - 1$.

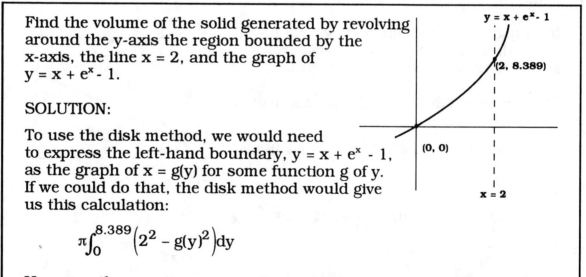

SOLUTION:

To use the disk method, we would need to express the left-hand boundary, $y = x + e^x - 1$, as the graph of x = g(y) for some function g of y. If we could do that, the disk method would give us this calculation:

$$\pi\int_0^{8.389} \left(2^2 - g(y)^2\right)dy$$

However, the equation $y = x + e^x - 1$ is difficult or impossible to solve for x, so we have no choice but to use the shell method.

For the shell method, we see from the diagram that:

a = 0
b = 2
c = 0
$f(x) = x + e^x - 1$
$g(x) = 0$

The calculation is then:

$$2\pi\int_0^2 (x-0)\left(x+e^x-1\right)dx$$

$$= 2\pi\int_0^2 \left(x^2 + xe^x - x\right)dx$$

$$= \left(\tfrac{1}{3}x^3 + xe^x - e^x - \tfrac{1}{2}x^2\right)\Big|_0^2$$

$$\approx 2\pi(9.0557)$$

$$\approx 56.898$$

(Integration by parts is required to antidifferentiate the xe^x term.)

Some problems are unkind enough to require 2 or more sub-regions regardless of whether we choose the washer or the shell method. In such cases, we use whichever approach appears easier at first glance.

EXAMPLE:

Find the volume of the solid which results from rotating the region bounded by $y = 2x$, $y = \tfrac{4}{5}x + \tfrac{6}{5}$, and $y = 12 - x$, around the line $y = -2$.

SOLUTION:

If we use the washer method, we will have to break the region up into two separate sub-regions as shown in the diagram:

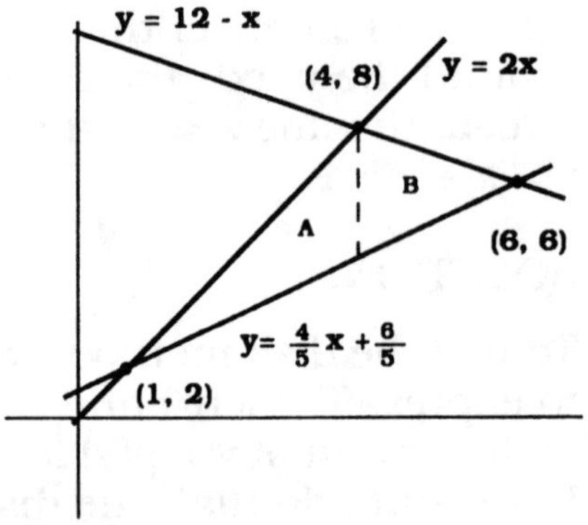

The washer method formula, in this case gives us:

$$\pi\int_1^4 \left[(2x-(-2))^2 - \left(\tfrac{4}{5}x + \tfrac{6}{5} - (-2)\right)^2\right]dx$$

$$+$$

$$\pi\int_4^6 \left[(12x-(-2))^2 - \left(\tfrac{4}{5}x + \tfrac{6}{5} - (-2)\right)^2\right]dx$$

$$= \pi\left(\tfrac{1836}{25} + \tfrac{1464}{25}\right)$$

$$= 132\pi$$

$$\approx 414.69$$

The shell method requires us to split the region into the two sub-regions shown in this diagram below:

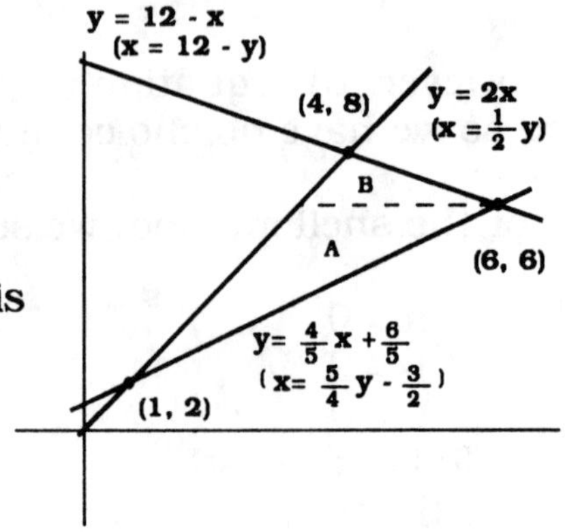

76

We also have to convert the equations of the boundaries to equations of x as a function of y:

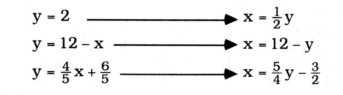

$$y = 2 \longrightarrow x = \tfrac{1}{2}y$$

$$y = 12 - x \longrightarrow x = 12 - y$$

$$y = \tfrac{4}{5}x + \tfrac{6}{5} \longrightarrow x = \tfrac{5}{4}y - \tfrac{3}{2}$$

The formula for the shell method gives:

$$2\pi\int_2^6 (y-(-2))\left(\left(\tfrac{5}{4}y - \tfrac{3}{2}\right) - \tfrac{1}{2}y\right)dy + 2\pi\int_6^8 (y-(-2))\left((12-y) - \tfrac{1}{2}y\right)dy$$

$$= 2\pi(40) + 2\pi(26)$$

$$= 132\pi$$

Finally, we give a summary of the criteria for deciding which method to use, and a list of the requirements for using each method.

Shell Method vs. Disk/Washer Method Criteria

<u>Around the x-axis or y = c:</u>	<u>Around the y-axis or x = c:</u>
Disk/Washer if:	Disk/Washer if:
The boundaries can be expressed as y = f(x) on top, y = g(x) on the bottom, x = a on the left, and x = b on the right.	The boundaries can be expressed as x = f(y) on the right, x = g(y) on the left, y = a on the bottom, and y = b on the top.
Shells if:	Shells if:
The boundaries can be expressed as x = f(y) on the right, x = g(y) on the left, y = a on the bottom, and y = b on the top.	The boundries can be expressed as y = f(x) on the top, y = g(x) on the bottom, x = a on the left, and x = b on the right.

Requirements for Disk or Washer Methods:

Around x-axis or y = c:	Around y-axis or x = c:
Upper and lower boundaries of region must be either graphs of y = some function of x, or horizontal lines (whose equations will have the form y = k for some number k).	Left and right boundaries of region must be either graphs of x = some function of y, or vertical lines (whose equations will have the form x = k for some number k).
Left and right boundaries of the region will be numerical values of x.	Upper and lower boundaries of the region will be numerical values of y.
Integration is done with respect to x:	Integration is done with respect to y:

$$\pi \int_a^b \left[\left(f(x) - c \right)^2 - \left(g(x) - c \right)^2 \right] dx$$

where a = left boundary of the
        region
   b = right boundary of the
        region
   c = taken from the equation
        of the axis of revolution,
        which is y = c. If the axis
        of revolution is the x-axis,
        then c = 0.
   $f(x)$ = upper boundary of the
        region.
   $g(x)$ = lower boundary of the
        region.

(If the region being revolved lies below the axis of revolution instead of above, the f(x) and the g(x) switch with each other).

Note that if the axis of revolution is the lower boundary of the region, then g(x) = c; hence in that case the expression (g(x) - c) in the integral formula simply drops out.

where a = lower boundary of the
        region
   b = upper boundary of the
        region
   c = taken from the equation
        of the axis of revolution,
        which is x = c. If the axis
        of revolution is the y-axis,
        then c = 0.
   $f(y)$ = right boundary of the
        region.
   $g(y)$ = left boundary of the
        region.

(If the region to be revolved lies to the left of the axis of revolution instead of to the right, then we switch the f(x) and the g(x)).

Note that if the axis of revolution is the left boundary of the region, then g(y) = c; hence in that case the expression (g(y) - c) in the integral formula simply drops out.

Requirements for Shell Method:

Around x-axis or y = c:

Right and left boundaries of region must be either graphs of x = some function of y, or vertical lines (whose equations will have the form x = k for some number k).

Upper and lower boundaries of the region will be numerical values of y.

Integration is done with respect to y:

$$2\pi\int_a^b (y - c)(f(y) - g(y))\,dy$$

where a = lower boundary of the region
      b = upper boundary of the region
      c = taken from the equation of the axis of revolution, which is y = c. If the axis of revolution is the x-axis, then c = 0.
    f(y) = right boundary of the region.
    g(y) = left boundary of the region.

(If the region to be revolved lies below the axis of revolution instead of above, then we switch the f(x) and the g(x)).

Around y-axis or x = c:

Lower and upper boundaries of region must be either graphs of y = some function of x, or horizontal lines (whose equations will have the form y = k for some number k).

Left and right boundaries of the region will be numerical values of x.

Integration is done with respect to x:

$$2\pi\int_a^b (x - c)(f(x) - g(x))\,dx$$

where a = left boundary of the region
      b = right boundary of the region
      c = taken from the equation of the axis of revolution, which is x = c. If the axis of revolution is the y-axis, then c = 0.
    f(x) = upper boundary of the region.
    g(x) = lower boundary of the region.

(If the region to be revolved lies to the left of the axis of revolution instead of to the right, then we switch the f(x) and the g(x)).

Definite Integrals. Exercise 8. Volumes of Solids-Shell Method

In all problems, use the method of your choice to calculate the volume of the solid which results from revolving the region with the given boundaries, around the given axis of revolution.

1. Boundaries: $\frac{1}{x}$, x-axis, x = 1, x = 10.
   Axis of revolution:
   a. y-axis
   b. x-axis
   c. x = -2
   d. y = -2

2. Boundaries: $y = x^4$, x = 1, y = 0.
   Axis of revolution:
   a. y-axis
   b. x-axis
   c. x = -1
   d. y = -2

3. Boundaries: xy = 4, y = 5 - x.
   Axis of revolution:
   a. x-axis
   b. y-axis
   c. y = 6
   d. x = 5

4. Boundaries: $y = x^2 - 4$, $y = 4 - x^2$.
   Axis of revolution:
   a. x = -2
   b. x = 3
   c. y = 4
   d. y = -6

Part 9 Acceleration, Velocity, and Distance

We learned in **Calculus AB, Volume 1** that if the position of an object is a function x(t) where t stands for time, then the velocity function v(t) is the derivative of x(t), and that the acceleration function a(t) is the derivative of the velocity function v(t), and therefore also the second derivative of x(t). Now that we have discovered antidifferentiation, the same facts may be stated backwards:

> v(t) is an antiderivative of a(t)

> x(t) is an antiderivative of v(t).

From these observations, we have a method for determining the functions v(t) and x(t) when we know a(t). We should note, however, that the "+ C" is always required when we find antiderivatives, and therefore a complete formula for v(t) or x(t) is impossible unless we have additional information.

Example:

> Suppose an object begins moving from a standing start, and the acceleration function for the object is:
>
> $$a(t) = \frac{1800}{(t+20)^2} \quad \text{for } 0 \le t \le 150.$$
>
> where the time is measured in seconds, and distance is measured in feet.

a. What is the velocity function for the object?

b. When will the object be moving at a velocity of 66 feet per second?

SOLUTION:

a. We know that the velocity function will be an antiderivative of

$a(t) = \dfrac{1800}{(t+20)^2}$, so we begin by finding $\int \dfrac{1800}{(t+20)^2}\,dt$, or $\int 1800(t+20)^{-2}\,dt$.

The answer, which is fairly easy to find, is: $-\dfrac{1800}{t+20} + C$.

However, this function is not terribly useful unless we know the value of C. We can find a value for C in this case, because the problem stated that the object begins from a standing start. That means that the velocity is zero when t = 0. That sentence can be translated into the equation:

$$0 = v(0) = \dfrac{-1800}{0+20} + C.$$

We can then solve the equation for C:

$$\dfrac{-1800}{20} + C = 0$$

$$C = \dfrac{1800}{20}$$

$$C = 90.$$

Now, substituting the value C = 90 into the formula for v(t), we finally get a completely determined function:

$$v(t) = 90 - \dfrac{1800}{t+20}.$$

b. Now that we have the velocity function, this question can be answered simply by setting v(t) = 66 and solving for t:

$$90 - \dfrac{1800}{t+20} = 66$$

$$90(t+20) - 1800 = 66(t+20)$$

$$t = 55.$$

Since the position function is an antiderivative of the velocity function, we can use ideas similar to those in the example above to solve problems dealing with the position of a moving object.

Example:

Suppose a particle is moving along the x-axis. When we begin our observations, the particle is located at x = 8, is moving left at 5 units per second, and its acceleration function is:

$$a(t) = \frac{1}{t+1}$$

a. Find the velocity of the particle at t = 5.
b. Find the position of the particle at t = 5.
c. At time t = 200, how far has the particle moved from its position at time y = 5?

SOLUTION:

a. As before, we find the velocity function by antidifferentiation, and calculate the constant from our knowledge of the velocity at time t = 0. We have:

$$v(t) = \int \frac{1}{t+1} dt$$
$$= \ln(t + 1) + C.$$

To find C, we note that the initial situation given in the problem is that v(0) = -5 (negative because the particle is moving to the left). So we solve for C:

$$\ln(0 + 1) + C = v(0) = -5$$

$$C = -5 \quad \text{(remember that the ln of 1 is 0)}$$

So the complete velocity function is:

$$v(t) = \ln(t + 1) - 5.$$

Therefore, $v(5) = \ln(5 + 1) - 5 \approx -3.208$.

b. To find the position function, we use the antiderivative of the velocity function, and again compute the constant from our knowledge of the initial position, which was x = 8. (Remember that the antiderivative of ln x is x (lnx) - x, as found in the discussion of integration by parts).

$$x(t) = \int (\ln(t + 1) - 5) dt$$
$$= (t + 1) \ln(t + 1) - (t + 1) - 5t + C$$
$$= (t + 1) \ln(t + 1) - 6t - 1 + C$$

From x(0) = 8, we get:

$$(0 + 1) \ln(0 + 1) - 6(0) - 1 + C = 8$$

and so C = 9.

The position function is then

$$x(t) = (t + 1) \ln(t + 1) - 6t - 1 + 9$$

$$\text{or } (t + 1) \ln(t + 1) - 6t + 8$$

Substituting $t = 5$, we get $x(5) = 6 \ln(6) - 6(5) + 8$, which is approximately -11.249.

c. First, let us note that the question does not ask for the total distance traveled by the particle between $t = 5$ and $t = 200$. That question would require us to find out the points at which the particle changes direction, and then add up the distances traveled between those points. In this case, all we have to do is to find out where the particle is at $t = 200$, and then calculate the distance between that point at the point $x = -11.249$, which is $x(5)$. So:

$$x(200) = (201) (\ln(201)) - 6(200) + 8$$

which is about -126.036. By subtraction, we see that at $t = 200$ the particle is about 114.787 units to the left of its position at $t = 5$.

It is worth noting that the answer to part c of the problem in the example above was $\int_2^{200} v(t)\, dt$. This gives us a useful formula:

The net change in position between $t = a$ and $t = b$ of an object whose velocity function is $v(t)$ is:

$$\int_a^b v(t)\, dt.$$

Definite Integrals. Exercise 9. Acceleration, Velocity, and Distance.

1. Suppose an object is moving up and down so that its acceleration function is $a(t) = 2t$ in inches per second per second. At time $t = 0$, the object is headed down at 4 inches per second, and is three feet high at the same time.

    a. Find the object's velocity at time $t = 6$.
    b. Find the object's position at time $t = 6$.
    c. Find the object's average velocity during the first 6 seconds.
    d. At what point in time does the object stop falling and begin rising?
    e. What is the lowest point the object will reach?

2. Suppose a particle is moving along the x-axis, beginning at $x = 5$, and suppose that the velocity function for the particle is $v(t) = 3t + \sin t$. Find the position and the acceleration of the particle at time $t = 10$.

3. An object is moving along a vertical line, beginning with a standing start at ground level. The acceleration function for the object is $a(t) = \frac{1}{t+1}$, where time is measured in seconds and distance in feet.

    a. Find the velocity function for the object.
    b. Find the position function for the object.
    c. How long will it take before the object reaches a velocity of 17.26664034 feet per second?

4. Suppose an object is moving along the x-axis in such a manner that its acceleration function is $a(t) = 3 \sin t$ for $0 \le t \le 2\pi$, where t is measured in minutes. Assume also that at time $t = \pi$, the velocity is 2 and the position is -3.

    a. what are the position and velocity of the object at $t = 0$?
    b. What is the position and velocity of the object at $t = 2\pi$?
    c. What is the average velocity of the object over the interval $[0, 2\pi]$?

5. Suppose the acceleration of an object is a constant -2, and suppose the average velocity of the object over the interval $0 \le t \le 10$ is 12. What is the velocity at time $t = 2$?

6. Suppose the acceleration function for an object is $a(t) = e^{.02t+1}$ and suppose the object starts from $x = 4$, moving left at 8 units per second.

    a. Find the velocity function v(t).
    b. Find the position function x(t).
    c. The object will cross the origin once between $t = 0$ and $t = 1$, and once again between $t = 5$ and $t = 6$. Use the Newton-Raphson Method to find those two values of t, to at least 3 places after the decimal point.
    d. What is the average velocity from $t = 0$ to $t = 10$?

Part 10 — Separable Differential Equations

A *differential* equation is an equation which contains one or more derivatives of y (possibly including second or third derivatives, or derivatives of any other order). The letter y is assumed to stand for some function of x. y' and y" are assumed to stand for the first and second derivatives of that function. A solution to the differential equation is not a numerical value, but rather an explicit formula for y as a function of x.

Example:

> The equation $y' + 3y = \frac{3x-1}{x^2}$ is a differential equation.
>
> The function $y = \frac{1}{x}$ is a solution to the equation, because if we substitute $y = \frac{1}{x}$ and $y' = \frac{-1}{x^2}$ (the derivative of $\frac{1}{x}$) into the differential equation, we get a true identity.

Perhaps the easiest kind of differential equation to solve is one which says nothing more than y' = g(x), where g(x) is some function of x. We can solve that equation by antidifferentiating g(x).

Example:

> Solve the differential equation y' = 2x - 3.
>
> SOLUTION:
>
> The solution is $y = \int (2x - 3)dx = x^2 - 3x + C$. In other words, $y = x^2 - 3x$, $y = x^2 - 3x + 1$, $y = x^2 - 3x - 223.7$, etc., are all possible solutions of the differential equation.

A differential equation is called separable if it can be written in the form:

$$y' \, f(y) = g(x)$$

where f(y) is any function of y, and g(x) is any function of x.

Example:

> (a) $3yy' = 5x$
>
> (b) $\frac{y'}{3y} = 5x$
>
> c) $(3y - 4e^y) \, y' = 5x - 2$
>
> (d) $3yy' = 5$
>
> (e) $3yy' = 4x + \frac{y'}{y+2}$
>
> (f) $y' = 6xy$
>
> (g) $y' \ln(y) = 4y \cos 6x$

85

The above are all separable differential equations which can be put into the form y' f(y) = g(x). In (a), we have f(y) = 3y, and g(x) = 5x. For the others, a little algebra is sometimes required, but we come up with the following:

	f(y)	g(x)
(b)	$\frac{1}{3y}$	5x
(c)	$3y - 4e^y$	5x-2
(d)	3y	5 (constant function)
(e)	$3y - \frac{1}{y+2}$	4x
(f)	$\frac{1}{y}$	6x
(g)	$\frac{\ln y}{4y}$	cos 6x

On the other hand, the differential equation

y' - 7y = 14x

is not separable, because there's nothing we can do which will change the left hand side into a y' times a function of y.

Once a separable differential equation is put into the form y' f(y) = g(x), the procedure for solving the equation is:

1. Replace y' with $\frac{dy}{dx}$.

2. Multiply both sides by the differential dx. That will give us
   f(y) dy = g(x) dx.

3. Integrate both sides. In other words, change the equation to
   $\int f(y)dy = \int g(x)dx$ and perform the antidifferentiation step on both sides.

4. Solve for y.

Examples:

Solve the following separable differential equations:

(a) $y^2 y' - x = 0$

(b) $y' = 6xy$

(c) $\frac{y'}{3y^2} = 2$

SOLUTIONS:

(a) Following the steps in the procedure above, we first rewrite the equation:
$$y^2 \, y' = x$$

Then replace the y' with $\frac{dy}{dx}$:
$$y^2 \frac{dy}{dx} = x$$

Then multiply both sides by dx:
$$y^2 dy = x \, dx$$

Then integrate both sides:
$$\int y^2 dy = \int x \, dx$$
$$\frac{y^3}{3} + C_1 = \frac{x^2}{2} + C_2$$

Now solve for y:
$$\frac{y^3}{3} = \frac{x^2}{2} + C_2 - C_1$$
$$y = \sqrt[3]{\frac{3x^2}{2} + 3(C_2 - C_1)}$$

However, C_2 and C_1 are arbitrary constants (they can be anything), so we can just let $C = 3(C_2 - C_1)$, which makes the final answer
$$y = \sqrt[3]{\frac{3x^2}{2} + C}.$$

(b) Following the same steps as before:
$$\frac{1}{y} \, y' = 6x$$
$$\frac{1}{y} \frac{dy}{dx} = 6x$$
$$\frac{1}{y} dy = \int 6x \, dx$$
$$\int \frac{1}{y} dy = \int 6x \, dx$$
$$\ln|y| + C_1 = 3x^2 + C_2$$
$$|y| = \pm e^{3x^2 + C_2 - C_1}$$
$$y = \pm e^{3x^2 + C_2 - C_1}$$
$$= \pm e^{3x^2} e^{C_2 - C_1}$$

Now we can let $C = e^{C_2 - C_1}$, which means C is any positive, *nonzero* number, and we have

$$y = \pm Ce^{3x^2}$$

But by allowing C to be either a positive or a negative nonzero number, we finally have

$$y = Ce^{3x^2}$$

(c) The equation is already in the form $y' f(y) = g(x)$, because 2 is a perfectly respectable (constant) function of x. So our steps are:

$$\frac{1}{3y^2}\frac{dy}{dx} = 2$$

$$\frac{1}{3}y^{-2}dy = 2dx$$

$$\frac{1}{3}\int y^{-2}dy = \int 2dx$$

$$-\frac{1}{3y} + C_1 = 2x + C_2$$

$$-\frac{1}{3} = y(2x + C_2 - C_1)$$

$$y = \frac{-1}{3(2x + C_2 + C_1)}$$

$$= \frac{-1}{6x + 3C_2 - 3C_1}$$

Finally, by setting $C = 3C_2 - 3C_1$, we have:

$$y = \frac{-1}{6x + C}$$

The solutions we found for the equations in the example above are sometimes referred to as *general* solutions, because the presence of a constant "C" means that we are expressing the form of an infinite number of possible solutions, one for each possible value of C. If we are given the value of y which corresponds to just one particular value of x, we can usually compute the value of C. Substituting that value for the "C" in the solution gives a *particular* solution to the equation.

Examples:

Find the particular solutions to the following differential equations:

(a) $y^2 y' - x = 0$, with $y(0) = 3$

(b) $y' = 6xy$, with $y(0) = -1$

(c) $\frac{y'}{3y^2} = 2$, with $y(1) = \frac{-1}{6}$

88

SOLUTIONS:

We already found the general solutions to these equations in the previous Example. All that remains is to find the value of C in each case.

(a) We already know that $y = \sqrt[3]{\frac{3x^2}{2}} + C$ for some constant C. We know also that $y(0) = 3$, which means that

$$y(0) = \sqrt[3]{\frac{3(0^2)}{2}} + C = 3$$
$$C = 27$$

Therefore, this particular solution to the equation is:

$$y = \sqrt[3]{\frac{3x^2}{2}} + 27$$

(b) From the previous example, we have the general solution:

$$y = Ce^{3x^2}$$

Now that we are given $y(0) = -1$, we solve the equation

$$y(0) = Ce^{3(0)} = -1$$

for C. We can see easily that the solution is $C = -1$; therefore the particular solution is:

$$y = (-1)e^{3x^2}, \text{ or } y = -e^{3x^2}$$

(c) The general solution, from the previous example, is:

$$y = \frac{-1}{6x+C}$$

From $y(0) = -\frac{1}{6}$, we get the equation

$$\frac{-1}{6(1)+C} = -\frac{1}{6}$$

which shows that $C = 0$. Therefore this particular solution to the differential equation is:

$$y = \frac{-1}{6x}.$$

Applications of Antiderivatives. Exercise 10. Separable Differential Equations.

In Problems 1-4, find the gneral solution to the differential equation.

1. $\dfrac{y'}{y^2} = x + 1$

2. $y' + 2 = \dfrac{1}{\sqrt{1-x^2}}$

3. $\dfrac{y'}{8y} = \dfrac{1}{3} y \sec^2 x$

4. $2y' = y(4x - 1)$

In problems 5-10, find the particular solution to the differntial equation.

5. $e^x = yy'$,　　$y(0) = 1$

6. $xe^x = yy'$,　$y(0) = 0$

7. $e^y y' = 5$,　$y(0) = 0$

8. $3xy' = 4y$,　　$y(1) = \pi$

9. $3y' = 2x + 7$,　$y(2) = 5$

10. $yy' = \ln x$,　$y(1) = 3$

Part 11 Growth and Decay

Recall that if two quantities Q and Q are *proportional* to each other, that means that the two quantities are related by the equation

$$Q = kQ$$

where k is a constant, sometimes called the constant of proportionality.

If a quantity y is increasing or decreasing at a rate proportional to the quantity itself, then we have the equation

$$y' = ky$$

where $y' = \dfrac{dy}{dt}$ is the rate of increase or decrease in y. Note that if k is positive, then y' will be positive, indicating that y is increasing as time progresses; a negative k means that y is decreasing. When k is positive, we call it the *growth constant*; when k is negative, we call it the *decay constant*.

The equation above is a separable differential equation, which can be solved using the methods of Part 10 (See particularly part (b) of the 4th example in Part 10). The solution to the equation is:

$$y = Ce^{kt}$$

where C might be any nonzero constant. Since the quantity y changes with time, y is a function of t. Threfeore we sometimes write the equation

$$y(t) = Ce^{kt}.$$

Note that when t = 0, we have

$$C = Ce^{k(0)} = y(0)$$

where $y(0)$ = the quantity y at time $t = 0$, or at the point in time from which we begin observing the change in y.

Example:

> Suppose a quantity Q is increasing with growth constant 0.2, and that $Q = 55$ when $t = 0$. Find the value of Q when $t = 8$.
>
> SOLUTION:
>
> According to the discussion above, the equation which allows us to compute Q for any value of t is:
>
> $$Q(t) = Q(0)e^{kt}$$
> $$= 55e^{0.2t}$$
>
> Therefore $Q(8) = 55e^{0.2(8)}$
> $$= 55(4.953)$$
> $$= 272.4.$$

Often, the growth or decay constant is unknown at the beginning of the problem. However, if we are given the value of the changing quantity at any two different points in time, we can calculate k for ourselves.

Example:

> An oil spill had caused the water in a certain area of the ocean to have 1200 parts per million (ppm) of polluting oil. One day later, the natural cleansing action of the ocean had reduced the pollution to 1170 ppm. Assuming that the rate of decrease in the concentration of oil is proportional to the concentration itself, how long will it take for the concentration to get down to 80 ppm?
>
> SOLUTION:
>
> Although the decay constant is not provided directly, we can figure it out by using the facts that $y(0) = 1200$ and $y(1) = 1170$ (where $y(t)$ is the concentration of the oil in the water at time t). The equation $y(0) = 1200$ tells us that the function $y(t)$ has the formula:
> $$y(t) = 1200e^{kt}$$
> where k is the decay constant. To find the value of k, we now substitute $t = 1$ and $y(1) = 1170$, and solve for k:
>
> $$1200e^{k(1)} = y(1) = 1170$$
> $$1200e^{k} = 1170$$
> $$e^{k} = \frac{1170}{1200}$$
> $$k = \ln\left(\frac{1170}{1200}\right)$$
> $$= -.0253178$$

Having found k, we proceed to set up an equation to answer the question in the problem. The question asks <u>when</u> the pollution will be down to 80 ppm, which means that the unknown is going to be t. Therefore, we need to have values for every other variable in the formula. We are given y(t) = 80, and we just calculated k = -.0253178. That is all we need; our equation is:

$$y(t) = 80 = 1200^{-.0253178t}$$

$$\frac{80}{1200} = e^{-.0253178t}$$

$$\ln\left(\frac{80}{1200}\right) = -.0253178t$$

$$\text{So } t = \frac{-2.7080502}{-.0253178}$$

$$= 107 \text{ (approximately)}$$

If interest is paid *continuously* on the principal in a financial account, that means that the rate of increase in the account is proportional to the amount in the account. In mathematical language, that means

$$A(t) = A(0)e^{rt}$$

where r = the interest rate. Remember that a percentage rate must be changed to a decimal number before using this formula (e.g., 5.3% would be converted to .053).

Example:

An account paying continuous interest at a rate of 5.2% has a balance of $1000 at the end of eight years. What was the original principal?

SOLUTION:

The unknown is the original principal, which is A(0). We are given values for the other variables in the formula, namely:

$$A(8) = 1000$$
$$r = .052$$
$$t = 8$$

So:

$$1000 = A(0)e^{.052(8)}$$

$$A(0) = \frac{1000}{e^{.416}}$$

$$= \$659.68.$$

Radioactive materials decay at a rate proportional to their quantity, and therefore the quantity at any point in time is defined by the formula

$$y(t) = y(0)e^{kt}.$$

The rate at which a radioactive element decays is usually given in terms of a *half-life*, which is the length of time it takes for <u>any</u> quantity of the material to decay down to half of its original quantity. Two important facts about a half-life are:

1. The half-life is a <u>length of time</u>, and therefore refers to the variable t in the formula. The half-life is not k, although we can use the half-life to calculate k, as we shall see below.

2. Unlikely as it may seem, the half-life is the amount of time it takes for *any* quantity of that material to decay down to half its orginal size. For example, if the half-life is 26 years, then 1000 grams will decay to 500 grams in 26 years, and 2 grams will decay to 1 gram in 26 years. Furthermore, 32 grams will decay to 16 grams in 26 years, thento 8 grams in another 26 years, and then to 4 grams in a third period of 26 years—78 years in all to decay from 32 grams to 4 grams.

Because of point #2 above, we can set up an equation showing the half-life by starting with any original quantity we want, although an original quantity of 1 will make life easiest.

Example:

A radioactive substance has a half-life of 481 years. Find the decay constant.

SOLUTION:

A half-life of 481 years implies that if y(0)=1, then y(481) = 0.5. So we can set up the standard decay equation with:

$$y(481) = .05$$
$$y(0) = 1$$
$$t = 481$$
$$k = \text{unknown}$$

So:

$$0.5 = 1e^{k(481)}$$

$$\ln(0.5) = 481k$$

$$k = \frac{\ln(0.5)}{481}$$

$$= -.001441$$

If we were to follow the procedure in the last example for any other half-life, we would find that the value of k is always given by:

$$k = \frac{\ln(0.5)}{\text{half-life}}$$

This formula can, of course, be solved for the half-life in terms of k also. That allows us to calculate the half-life if we know the value of k, as called for in one of the exercises to follow.

Definite Integrals. Exercise 11. Growth and Decay.

1. The population of Alabama was 2,646,248 in 1930, and 3,061,743 in 1950. Assume that the population has always grown and will always grow at the same relative rate.

    a. What was the population in 1965?
    b. What was the population in 1920?
    c. When did (or will) the population reach 4,000,000?
    d. When was the population exactly one?

2. A financial account pays 4.8% compounded continuously. The initial value of the account is $500.

    a. What will be the value of the account in 10 years?
    b. What would be the value of the account in 10 years if we had only simple interest, according to the formula I = PRT?
    c. How long will it take the account to double in value (with continuous compounding)?

3. A bacteria culture doubles its population every 2.5 hours. There are 1000 bacteria at   12:00 noon.

    a. How many bacteria will there be at 8:00 PM?
    b. When will there be 1,000,000 bacteria?

4. A radioactive material decays at a rate such that 100 grams becomes 85 grams in 50 years.

    a. What is the half-life?
    b. How much (of an initial 100 grams) will be left in 123 years?
    c. How long will it take for the 100 grams to decay to 5 grams?

5. The half-life of a radioactive element is 35 days.

    a. If t is expressed in days, what is the decay constant?
    b. If we start with 50 grams, how much is left after 10 days?
    c. If we start with 50 grams, how long will it take before there are 10 grams left?

6. A bacteria culture has a population of 1500 at midnight. By 6:00AM there are 10,000 bacteria.

    a. If t is expressed in hours, what is the growth constant?

    b. How long does it take the population to double? (Give answer in hours, minutes, and seconds.

    c. At what time will there be 20,000 bacteria? DO THIS PART WITHOUT A CALCULATOR.

7.   a. What rate of interest, compounded continuously, must be paid in order for money to double in 12 years.

    b. If money doubles in 12 years with interest paid continuously, how long does it take for the value of the account to be multiplied by 2.5?

8. The population of Goontown doubles every 30 years. The population was 7500 on January 1, 1980.

    a. What is the January 1, 1994 population?

    b. On what date will the population be 75,000?

Answers

Antiderivatives. Exercise 1. Page 5-6.

1. $e^{x+2} + C$

2. $2\cos^{-1}x + C$

3. $\frac{2\sqrt{x^3}}{9} + C$

4. $-\frac{3}{5}\ln|x| + C$

5. $2e^{\frac{x}{2}-6} + C$

6. $\frac{4}{5}\tan^{-1}x + C$

7. $3x^{\frac{1}{3}} + C$

8. $\frac{x^6}{24} + C$

9. $\frac{3}{5}\tan x + C$

10. $\frac{2}{5}\sqrt{x^5} + C$

11. $e\ln|x| + C$

12. $-\frac{1}{2}x^{12} + C$

13. $\frac{-\cos x}{4} + C$

14. $\frac{-1}{6x^4} + C$

15. $\ln|x| + C$

16. $\frac{-2x^5}{35} + C$

17. $\sec^{-1}x + C$

18. $\frac{21}{4}x^{\frac{4}{3}} + C$

19. $-\frac{1}{5}\ln|x| + C$

20. $\csc x + C$

21. $\frac{1}{x^2} + C$

22. $\frac{-8x^{-\frac{1}{4}}}{5} + C$

23. $-\frac{4}{3}e^{\frac{3}{2}} - 8 + C$

24. $-\frac{1}{4}x^{-4} + C$

25. $12x^{\frac{1}{3}} + C$

26. $\frac{x^2}{2} + C$

27. $-2\tan x + C$

28. $\frac{-1}{9x^3} + C$

29. $\frac{6}{5\sqrt[3]{x}} + C$

30. $\frac{1}{7}e^{7x+\pi} + C$

31. $\frac{1}{2}\sin^{-1}x + C$

32. $\frac{7x^{\frac{12}{5}}}{12} + C$

33. $2\tan^{-1}x - 3\ln|x + C|$

34. $\frac{4e^{\frac{1}{4}x-2}}{3} - \frac{3}{4}x^{-\frac{4}{3}} + C$

35. $-\frac{2}{3}\sin t + \ln|t| + C$

36. $x^5 + \frac{2}{3x^2} + C$

37. $\frac{y^3}{15} + \frac{2y^2}{5} - \frac{6\sqrt{y}}{5} + \frac{2}{5}\ln|y| + C$

38. $-x^{-1} + 8\sqrt{x} - \frac{x^3}{3} + C$

39. $-2\cos t - \frac{1}{6t^2} + \frac{2}{5\sqrt{t^3}} + C$

40. $-\frac{e^{5x}}{5} + \frac{\tan^{-1}x}{3} + \frac{\sqrt[3]{x^4}}{6} + C$

Antiderivatives. Exercise 2. Page 8.

1. $f(x) = -3x + 1$

2. $f(x) = e^x - 1$

3. $f(x) = 4\ln|x| + 2x - 2$

4. $f(x) = 3\tan x - \frac{x^2}{2} + .55511959$

5. $f(x) = \frac{3}{8}x^2 + 7x + 44$

6. $f(x) = \frac{x^2}{200} - 33$

7. $f(x) = \frac{x^3}{300} - \frac{9949}{3}$

8. $f(x) = .01\left(\frac{x^3}{3} - \frac{x^2}{2}\right) - \frac{9799}{3}$

9. $f(x) = \tan^{-1}x + 2$

10. $f(x) = \frac{e^{2x-2}}{2} + \frac{3x^2}{2} - 2 - \frac{e^2}{2}$

$\quad\quad = \frac{e^{2x-2}}{2} + \frac{3x^2}{2} - 5.694528049$

Antiderivatives. Exercise 3. Page 14.

1. $\frac{1}{4}(\sin x - x\cos x) + C$

2. $-xe^{-x} - e^{-x} + C$

3. $\frac{1}{5}\left(2e^{2x}\cos x + e^{2x}\sin x\right) + C$

4. $(3x - 1)\sin x + 3\cos x + C$

5. $x^2\ln x - \frac{1}{2}x^2 + C$

6. $(1 + \ln 2)x - x\ln x + C$?? $x\ln(\frac{x}{2}) + x + C$

7. $\frac{1}{10}\left(x\cos(\ln(x^3)) + 3x\sin(\ln(x^3))\right) + C$

8. $-\frac{1}{10}\left(e^{-3x}\cos x + 3e^{-3x}\sin x\right) + C$

9. $x\left(\left(\ln\frac{5}{3}\right) - 2\right) + 2x\ln x + C$? $x\,\text{IN}\left(\frac{5x^2}{3}\right) - 2x + C$

10. $\frac{x^2e^{3x}}{3} - \frac{2xe^{3x}}{9} + \frac{2e^{3x}}{27} + C$

11. $\frac{1}{2}(x + \sin x\cos x) + C$

12. $\frac{1}{4}(t + \sin t\cos t - 2t\cos^2 t) + C$

13. $\int \cos^{2n}x\, dx =$

$\quad\quad \frac{1}{2n}\left(\sin x\cos^{2n-1}x + (2n - 1)\int\cos^{2n-2}x\, dx\right)$

Antiderivatives. Exercise 4. Page 21.

1. $\ln\left(x^2 - 3x + 5\right) + C$

2. $\sin(e^x) + C$

3. $-e^{\sin x} + C$

4. $\frac{1}{2}\left(x^2 + x - 8\right)^{46} + C$

5. $\frac{1}{3}\sin^3(2x + 1) + C$

6. $\ln|\tan x| + C$

7. $\frac{1}{3}\ln|\tan x| + C$

8. $x + 1 + \ln|x + 1| + C$ or

$\quad x + \ln|x + 1| + C$.

$\quad$ Why are the answers equivalent?

9. $\frac{(x+1)^2}{2} - 2x + 3\ln|x + 1| + C$

10. $\sqrt{x^2 - 3x + 8} + C$

11. $\frac{-1}{\sqrt{e^{2t} + 4t^2}} + C$

12. $\tan(\ln x) + C$

13. $-\frac{1}{2}\cos^2(\ln x) + C$ or

$\quad \frac{1}{2}\sin^2(\ln x) + C$

$\quad$ Why are the answers equivalent?

14. $-\cos\left[(\ln x)^2\right] + C$

15. $\left(2x - \frac{4}{3}\right)\ln(3x - 2) - 2x + C$

$\quad$ See note on answer #8.

16. $\frac{-1}{2e^{\tan^2 x}} + C$

17. $\frac{1}{2}\tan(e^{2x}) + C$

18. $\frac{1}{6}\left(-\cos\left(2r^3 - 3r^2 + 4\right) - e^{2r^3 - 3r^2 + 4}\right) + C$

19. $\frac{\cos^3 x}{3} - \cos x + C$

20. $-\frac{1}{125}\left(32(4 - 5x)^{\frac{3}{2}} - \frac{48}{5}(4 - 5x)^{\frac{5}{2}} + \frac{6}{7}(4 - 5x)^{\frac{7}{2}}\right) + C$

21. $\left(2x^2 + 5x - 1\right)^4 - 5$

22. $e^{\sin x} - 1.6487$ $\left(\text{or } e^{\sin x} - \sqrt{e}\right)$

23. $\frac{(ax+b)^{n+1}}{a(n+1)} + C$

24. $\sin^{-1}\left(\frac{x}{a}\right) + C$

25. $-\ln|\cos x| + C$

26. $\ln|\sin x| + C$

Antiderivatives. Exercise 5. Page 26.

1. $e^{\tan x} + C$

2. $\ln\left|e^x + 5x^3\right| + C$

3. $\ln|\ln x| + C$

4. $\frac{4}{3}xe^{3x} - \frac{4}{9}e^{3x} + C$

5. $2x^2 e^{3x} - \frac{4}{3}xe^{3x} + \frac{4}{9}e^{3x} + C$

6. $e^{e^x} + C$

7. $\sin(\sin x) + C$

8. $\frac{5}{26}e^{5x-1}\sin x - \frac{1}{26}e^{5x-1}\cos x$

9. $-\sin(\cos x) + C$

10. $x\tan^{-1}x - \frac{1}{2}\ln\left(1 + x^2\right) + C$

11. $-\frac{4}{3}\left[\left(2 - \frac{3}{4}x\right)\tan^{-1}\left(2 - \frac{3}{4}x\right) + \frac{2}{3}\ln\left(1 + \left(2 - \frac{3}{4}x\right)^2\right)\right] + C$

12. $\tan^{-1}(\ln x) + C$

13. $\ln\left|x + \sqrt{x^2 - 1} + C\right|$

14. $2\sqrt{\sin x - e^{3x} + 4x^5 - 8x + 1}$

15. $-\frac{1}{20}\cos^2\left(5x^2 - 4\right) + C$

16. $x\cos^{-1}x - \sqrt{1 - x^2} + C$

17. $\frac{5}{21}\sin 2x \sin 5x + \frac{2}{21}\cos 2x \cos 5x + C$

18. $\frac{b}{b^2 - a^a}\sin ax \sin bx + \frac{a}{b^2 - a^a}\cos ax \cos bx + C$

Antiderivatives. Exercise 6. Page 34.

1. $2\ln|x - 1| + 3\ln|x + 1| + C$

2. $\frac{2}{3}\ln|x - 1| - \frac{4}{5}\ln|x + 1| + C$

3. $\ln|x| - 5\ln|x + 2| + \frac{3}{4}\ln|x + 5| + C$

4. $5\ln|x + 2| - \frac{1}{3}\ln|x| - 3\ln|x + 5| + C$

5. $2\ln|x| - \frac{3}{x} - \ln|x - 10| + C$

6. $-\frac{3}{x} - \ln|x - 10| + C$

7. $4\ln|x + 1| - \frac{5}{2(x+1)} + C$

8. $\frac{3}{2}x^2 + 8x + 2\ln|x| - \frac{8}{3}\ln|x - 5| + C$

9. $\frac{2}{3}x^3 - 3x + 2\ln|x - 1| + \frac{8}{3x} + C$

10. $\frac{2}{3}x^3 - 3x + \frac{48}{5}\ln|x - 1| + \frac{4}{5}\ln|x| + \frac{1}{3x} + C$

98

Antiderivatives. Exercise 6. (con't)

11. $5\ln|x-4| + 4\ln|x+4| - \frac{3}{2}\ln|x+1| + \frac{2}{3}\ln|x-1| + C$

12. $3\ln|5x-4| - \frac{3}{10(5x-4)} - 7\ln|x| + C$

13. $5\ln x + \frac{6}{x} - 3\ln|x+1| - \frac{1}{x+1} + C$

14. $5\ln x - \frac{6}{x} + \frac{3}{2x^2} + \ln|x=1| + C$

15. $\frac{1}{5}\ln|x-7| - \frac{1}{5}\ln|x-2| + C$

16. $\frac{3}{8}\ln|x-4| - \frac{3}{8}\ln|x+4| + C$

Miscellaneous Integration. Exercise 7. Page 34.

1. $e^x + 3x + \frac{5}{e^x} + C$

2. $-x\cos x + \sin x + \cos x + C$

3. $\frac{x^3}{4} + \frac{1}{\sqrt{x}} + \frac{5x}{4} + \frac{3}{4x} + C$

4. $\left(\frac{5x^6}{6} + \frac{4x^5}{5} - \frac{3x^4}{4}\right)\ln x - \frac{5x^6}{36} - \frac{4x^5}{25} + \frac{3x^4}{16} + C$

5. $x^2 - 5x - \frac{2}{3x+3} - 5\ln|x-2| + C$

6. $2x\sin x + 2\cos x - x^2\cos x + C$

7. $\frac{-2}{3x+3} - 5\ln|x-2| + C$

8. $\frac{1}{2}x^2\arcsin x^2 + \frac{1}{2}\left(1-x^4\right)^{\frac{1}{2}} + C$

9. $x + 5\ln|x-2| - 2\ln(x-1) + C$

10. $e^{\sin(3x^2-4x)} + C$

11. $3\ln|x-2| - 2\ln|x-1| + C$

12. $\ln|\sin x - \tan x| + C$

13. $\ln|x-2| - \ln|x-1| + C$

14. $-\frac{1}{6}\cos^3\left(3x^2+2x+1\right) + C$

15. $\frac{-x^2-3}{x^2+1} + \ln\left|x^2+1\right| + C$

16. $-\frac{1}{2}\cos\left(3x^2+2x+1\right) + C$

17. $\left(2x^2-6\right)\sin\left(x^2-3\right) + 2\cos\left(x^2-3\right)...$

$$...-\left(x^2-3\right)^2\cos\left(x^2-3\right) + C$$

18. $2\tan^{-1}(4-3x) + C$

19. $\frac{-x^2}{e^x} - \frac{2x}{e^x} - \frac{2}{e^x} + C$

20. $\ln\left|\sin(e^{4x^2-\tan x})\right| + C$

Definite Integrals. Exercise 1. Page 43.

1. 10.29965		**14.** -5.95342	
2. -96016		**15.** -27.65776	
3. $-\frac{8}{3}$		**16.** 0.32994	
4. -3.71239		**17.** -5.71328	
5. -219,802,125.6		**18.** 800	
6. 1.68294		**19.** -2.57944	
7. 3.20664		**20.** 0	
8. 1.84444		**21.** 14.53654	
9. 14.30227		**22.** 17.52146	
10. -0.37528		**23.** 0.72244	
11. 0.5		**24.** 0.1182	
12. 134.14293		**25.** 4	
13. -0.23112		**26.** -8	

Definite Integrals. Exercise 2. Page 46.

1. 55

2. -40

3. 189

4. $\frac{100}{101}$

5. $1 + \frac{1}{2} - \frac{1}{101} - \frac{1}{102}$, or $\frac{7625}{5151}$

6. $\frac{7625}{5151}$

7. 5

8. $\frac{1023}{1024}$

9. $\sum_{k=3}^{1234} k$, or $\sum_{k=1}^{1232} (x+2)$

10. $\sum_{k=2}^{617} 2k$

11. $\sum_{k=1}^{11} \frac{2}{3^k}$

12. $\sum_{k=1}^{10} (-1)^{k+1}\left(\frac{2}{3}\right)^k$, or $-\sum_{k=1}^{10}\left(-\frac{2}{3}\right)^k$

Definite Integrals. Exercise 3. Page 50.

1. **a.** 9
   b. 36
   c. 19.125

2. **a.** 14.0625
   b. 27.5625
   c. 19.96875

3. **a.** 4.3125
   b. 20.3125
   c. 9.85156

4. **a.** 9.24618
   b. 35.18611
   c. 15.89539

5. **a.** 1.89189
   b. 1.13509
   c. 1.72461

6. **a.** 1.95409
   b. 1.95409
   c. 2.02303

7. **a.** 12.13996
   b. 15.59384
   c. 14.10197

8. **a.** 4.37309
   b. 4.03975
   c. 4.19265

9. **a.** 0.33876
   b. 1.39712
   c. 0.70213

10. **a.** 48.59231
    b. 56.48221
    c. 52.53091

Definite Integrals. Exercise 4. Page 56-57.

1. Midpoint: 2.326096
   Trapezoidal: 2.399166
   Simpson's: 2.350453
   Actual: 2.350402

2. Midpoint 20.9375
   Trapezoidal: 21.125
   Simpson's: 21
   Actual: 21

3. Midpoint: -0.336910
   Trapezoidal: -0.335227
   Simpson's: -0.336349
   Actual: -0.336349

4. Midpoint: 2.017048
   Trapezoidal: 1.994366
   Simpson's: 2.009487
   Actual: 2.009492

5. Midpoint: 9.670049
   Trapezoidal: 9.564882
   Simpson's: 9.634994
   Actual: 9.635532

6. Midpoint: -31.79388
   Trapezoidal: -33.21015
   Simpson's: -32.26597
   Actual: -32.26482

7. Midpoint: 1.080573
   Trapezoidal: 0.816012
   Simpson's: 0.992386

8. Midpoint: 3.513173
   Trapezoidal: 3.536928
   Simpson's: 3.521091

9. Midpoint: 1055.8037
   Trapezoidal: 2319.0715
   Simpson's: 1476.8929

10. Midpoint: 76.125347
    Trapezoidal: 78.250841
    Simpson's: 76.833845

11. Midpoint: 3.602865
    Trapezoidal: 3.614573
    Simpson's: 3.606768

12. Midpoint: -0.930732
    Trapezoidal: -1.029970
    Simpson's: -0.963811

13. Midpoint: 1.167309
    Trapezoidal: 1.244737
    Simpson's: 1.193119

14. Midpoint: -0.671381
    Trapezoidal: 86.768957
    Simpson's: 28.475399

The answers are meaningless because the given function is not continuous on the interval [2,5]. The denominator, $\cos(2x+1)$, is zero when $x = \frac{5\pi}{4} - \frac{1}{2}$, or 3.427.

Definite Integrals. Exercise 5. Page 61.

1. 32.3056
2. 0.4548
3. 21.333
4. 42
5. 57.1667
6. 4
7. 14.6667
8. 27.6977
9. 21.3333
10. 3.7712
11. 90.3472
12. 43.0770
13. 8
14. 27

Definite Integrals. Exercise 6. Page 63.

1. 0.0735
2. 1835.53
3. 53.4263
4. -0.5536
5. 459.25
6. -0.482048, not continuous at x = 2.
7. 2.16667
8. 0.164088
9. 5.338879
10. 7.915375

Definite Integrals. Exercise 7. Page 71-72.

1. $\pi\ln 9 \approx 6.90$

2. $9\pi \approx 28.27$

3. $2\pi \approx 6.28$

4. $\frac{320\pi}{3} \approx 335.10$

5. $2\pi \approx 6.28$

6. $\frac{16\pi}{3} \approx 16.76$

7. $\frac{16\pi}{3} \approx 16.76$

8. $\frac{81\pi}{2} \approx 127.23$

9. $\frac{972\pi}{5} \approx 610.73$

10. $\frac{207\pi}{2} \approx 325.15$

11. $\frac{1332\pi}{5} \approx 836.92$

12. $\frac{65\pi}{2} \approx 102.1$

13. $\frac{1012\pi}{5} \approx 211.95$

14. $\frac{296\pi}{5} \approx 185.98$

15. $\frac{565\pi}{6} \approx 295.83$

16. $\frac{(e^4-1)\pi}{2} \approx 84.19$

17. $\left(2e^2 + 2\right)\pi \approx 52.71$

18. $\left(6e^2 - 2\right)\pi \approx 133.00$

19. $\left(16e^2 - \frac{e^4+31}{2}\right)\pi \approx 236.96$

20. $\frac{72\pi}{5} \approx 45.24$

21. $\frac{45\pi}{2} \approx 70.69$

22. a. $\frac{64}{15}$ **b.** $\frac{16}{3}$ **c.** $\frac{16\sqrt{3}}{5}$

Definite Integrals. Exercise 8. Page 80.

1. **a.** $18\pi \approx 56.549$
   b. $.9\pi \approx 2.827$
   c. 85.484
   d. 31.76

2. **a.** $\frac{\pi}{3} \approx 1.047$
   b. $\frac{\pi}{9} \approx 0.349$
   c. $\frac{11\pi}{15} \approx 2.304$
   d. $\frac{41\pi}{45} \approx 2.862$

3. **a.** $9\pi \approx 28.274$
   b. $9\pi \approx 28.274$
   c. 45.421
   d. 33.138

4. **a.** $\frac{256\pi}{3} \approx 268.083$
   b. $128\pi \approx 402.124$
   c. $\frac{512\pi}{3} \approx 536.165$
   d. $256\pi \approx 804.248$

Definite Integrals. Exercise 9. Page 83-84.

1. **a.** 32 inches per second.
   b. 7 feet (84 inches) high
   c. 8 inches per second
   d. $t = 2$
   e. 30.67 inches high

2. Position: 156.839
   Acceleration: 2.161

3. **a.** $\ln(t + 1)$
   b. $(t + 1) \ln (t + 1) - t$
   c. 1 year (31,536,000 seconds)

4. **a.** Position: $\pi - 3 \approx 0.1416$
      Velocity: -4
   b. Position: $-3 - \pi \approx -6.1416$
      Velocity: -4
   c. -1

5. 18

6. **a.** $50e^{.02t+1} - 143.914$
   b. $2500e^{.02t+1} - 143.914t - 6791.705$
   c. 0.55195 and 5.13244
   d. 6.5447

Definite Integrals. Exercise 10. Page 90.

1. $y = \frac{-2}{x^2+2x+C}$

2. $y = \sin^{-1}x - 2x + C$

3. $y = \frac{-3}{8\tan x+C}$

4. $y = Ce^{x^2 - \frac{1}{2}x}$

5. $y = \sqrt{2e^x - 1}$

6. $y = \pm\sqrt{2xe^x - 2e^x + 2}$

7. $y = \ln(5x + 1)$

8. $y = \pi x^{\frac{4}{3}}$

9. $y = \frac{x^2+7x-3}{3}$

10. $y = \sqrt{2x\ln x - 2x + 11}$

Definite Ingegrals. Exercise 11. Page 94.

1. **a.** 3,415,642
   b. 2,460,149
   c. Late 1986
   d. 98 BC

2. **a.** $808.04
   b. $740.00
   c. 14.44 years

3. **a.** 9190
   b. 12 : 54 : 52 PM the next day

4. **a.** 213.25 years
   b. 67.05 grams
   c. 921.66 years

5. **a.** – 0.019804
   b. 41.02 grams
   c. 81.267483 days
      (81 days, 6 hours, 25 minutes, 11 seconds)

6. **a.** 0.3161867
   b. 2 hours, 11 minutes, 32 seconds
   c. 8 : 11 : 32 AM

7. **a.** 5.776%
   b. 15.863 years, or 15 years, 315 days

8. **a.** 10,364
   b. Mid 2079 (August 28, 2079)